THE GODDESS IN THE GOSPELS

The GODDESS in the GOSPELS

Reclaiming the Sacred Feminine

MARGARET STARBIRD

Bear & Company
One Park Street
Rochester, Vermont 05767
www.InnerTraditions.com

Bear & Company is a disvision of Inner Traditions International

Library of Congress Cataloging-in-Publication Data

Starbird, Margaret, 1942-
    The goddess in the Gospels : reclaiming the sacred feminine / Margaret Starbird.
        p. cm.
    Includes bibliographical reference and index.
    ISBN 1-879181-48-7
    1. Starbird, Margaret, 1942-   —Religion.   2. Mary Magdalene, Saint—Miscellanea.   3. Jesus Christ—Miscellanea.   4. Mary Magdalene, Saint—Marriage.   5. Jesus Christ—Marriage   I. Title.
BX4705.S8123A3   1998
232.9—dc21   98-28283
                                                                                   CIP

Editing: Barbara Doern Drew
Typesetting: Melinda Belter
Cover illustration © 1998 by Sarah Honeycutt-Steele
Cover Design: Beth Hansen-Winter

9 8 7

For my parents,
Charles Frederick Leonard, Jr.,
and
Margery Beukema Leonard,
who were married in a garden
and whose union blessed so many lives.

CONTENTS

Acknowledgments ix
Preface xi

Poem. To Our Lady 3
CHAPTER I. Pilgrim in Provence 5
CHAPTER II. Bound on Earth 13
CHAPTER III. The Dark Bride 29
CHAPTER IV. The Community Emmanuel 41
CHAPTER V. The Destroying Mountain 53
CHAPTER VI. Our Lady of the Quest 65
CHAPTER VII. The Fall of Babylon 81
CHAPTER VIII. Harrowing Hell 93
CHAPTER IX. Magdalene's Legacy 111
CHAPTER X. The Lord of the Fishes 123
CHAPTER XI. A New Song 137
CHAPTER XII. The Sacred Reunion 145

Appendix 1 155
Appendix 2 157
Appendix 3 159
Appendix 4 161
Notes 165
Selected Bibliography 171
Index 175
About the Author 181

ACKNOWLEDGMENTS

Since the publication of my first book, friends of that work have encouraged me to tell the story of my personal quest for the lost feminine in Christianity. In the beginning, I had no idea that I would find her at the heart of the Gospels I loved. But even in the beginning, she was there.

I would like to thank all those who have contacted me after reading *The Woman with the Alabaster Jar*. Their overwhelmingly positive response to my work has given me the courage to commit the story of my search to writing.

My husband and our children have been a continual source of support and encouragement over these many years of my journey. Because my first commitment was to feeding the hungry and clothing the naked under my own roof, they have helped to keep me grounded in reality, living in the moment. They have also helped me separate the wheat from the chaff in my search for truth. They are an integral part of my spiritual path, which at times has been a difficult assignment. I am greatly in their debt and thank them for enriching my life in so many ways!

The members of the Emmanuel community nurtured and supported me with their prayers and insights along the path. This book could never have been written without their help. In particular, I want to express my gratitude to Mary Beben, who wrestled with the revelations we received and who spent countless hours editing material included in this volume. Her profound insights and suggestions have been invaluable in shaping my work, and her friendship has blessed my life and my spiritual journey.

The editors at Bear and Company have given me tremendous assistance in preparing the present manuscript. Barbara Hand Clow offered encouragement and invaluable suggestions that helped me plumb the depths of my own story, and Barbara Doern Drew and

Gerry Clow have been tireless in polishing and honing the final product. I wish also to thank Richard Freeman Allan of JBL Statues for the Magdalene figurine that helped to inspire the cover design and Sara Honeycutt-Steele for the radiant image of Magdalene that graces the cover of the book.

I have been richly blessed by all those who have shared my journey—fellow pilgrims, both family and friends, and those who have attended my workshops and lectures around the United States and in Europe. Their enthusiasm for my belief that Magdalene and Christ were the archetypal Bride and Bridegroom of the Christian mythology has supplied a deep well from which I have drawn continuous support in my attempt to reclaim the Goddess in the Gospels.

P R E F A C E

This story is stranger than fiction. It is the story of a surprising spiritual journey, the years I spent searching for the lost Grail of the European legends, and the final realization that it was not an artifact I was searching for, but a woman, the lost bride of Jesus.

Friends of *The Woman with the Alabaster Jar* have asked me to publish the story of my quest for the Sacred Marriage that was once at the very heart of Christianity, of how I stumbled upon the devastating flaw in the foundation of the Church—the scorned and repudiated feminine—and why, after so many years of being a conservative and very orthodox daughter of the Roman Catholic Church, I am singing a new song. This volume is offered as a response to their request. The path has been sometimes dark, even terrifying at times, the footing often treacherous. But I am finally ready to commit the story of my quest to writing because it is important that the hidden version of the Christian story survive.

At first, I was reluctant to hear about the marriage of Jesus because the idea was so contrary to everything I had been taught. I was reluctant to examine the evidence for it and later reluctant to speak of it. But that fear has subsided now. Because of the way the story has unfolded, step by step, aided by incredible gifts of synchronicity, I am now persuaded that all of reality is interwoven, a fabulous tapestry of silken threads linked with tiny knots behind the fabric.

Details of the quest for the Grail seem to have been carefully interconnected in my unconscious. Many favorite childhood memories played a role, illuminating dark corners of my mind like candle flames in the night. Blue iris and stone citadels, beloved fairy tales, storybook titles, symbols, and puns became vehicles for the unfolding of the myth, helping it break into consciousness. It was as if now and then I was permitted a glimpse of the completed embroidered tapestry from the front, instead of always seeing the reverse side where the multicolored threads are crisscrossed back and forth in an intricate but meaningless web.

Inextricably interwoven with my search for the Grail is the story of Emmanuel, a charismatic community formed in 1974 and consecrated by a Roman Catholic priest at a special liturgy in May 1979 as intercessors for the purification and healing of the Roman Catholic Church and her priesthood. The specific vehicles of the prophetic revelations we received were many: timely Scripture passages, locutions, and often startling synchronicities. Sudden enlightenment was once the role of Hermes, the guardian of the crossroads, messenger of the gods. Among Christians, the orchestrating of meaningful coincidence is attributed to the Holy Spirit, who traditionally guides, illumines, and comforts the pilgrim on life's journey.

This intricate "networking" is one of the traditional roles of the "Paraclete"—from the Greek word meaning, appropriately, "traveling companion." Whereas God the Father/Creator is honored as the transcendent principle—enthroned in glory somewhere "out there" and unforgettably painted on the ceiling of the Sistine Chapel in the Vatican, the Holy Spirit is the immanent "feminine" aspect of the Divine, ever guiding us from within. She is both weaver and teacher—Holy Wisdom herself. Over the years, it has been the uncanny and sometimes overwhelming "coincidences" and "synchronicities" that have guided my steps, leading me deeper into the truth stored in the cells of my own body as well as in the dusty volumes of libraries.

An additional significant source of revelation for me was the ancient canon of sacred geometry and a numerical system known as *gematria*, in which alphabet letters were used as numbers which carried symbolic meaning.[1] This system was widely practiced by both Hebrew and Greek authors and was especially popular during the Hellenistic period when the Gospels were written. In the wake of Michael Drosnin's book *The Bible Code*[2] with its startling evidence of codes found in the Torah of Judaism, it should not be considered too surprising that the New Testament is also coded. *Gematria* was a hidden dimension of enlightenment for those who held the key. The authors of the New Testament knew that the Hebrew Scriptures were coded and, although they could not decipher them, they decided to encode their own sacred texts of the New Covenant as well.

In their pursuit of the historical Jesus of Nazareth, some Scripture scholars have played down the strong influence of Hellenistic culture and classical philosophy on the first several centuries of the Christian movement. Jesus was a charismatic Jewish teacher, but the texts of the New Testament were written in Greek and their interpretation is greatly enhanced by the classical Greek form of *gematria*. Illumination I received from the numbers encoded in the New Testament was profound, the interplay of these various sources providing me with a wealth of surprising information—treasures from out of the darkness. Specific explanations of New Testament gematria are to be found in appendices 1 through 3 of this volume.

I feel it is important now to share this prophetic material, gleaned over the years from myriad sources, as it directly relates to the restoring of the Bride to the Christian story, and in the process, to each of us and to our world as well.

Jesus was born into Judaism and came "to fulfill the law," but from its beginnings the Christian community has had many, sometimes incompatible, interpretations of the life and words of the master. It is my hope that those who read my revision of the Christian story to include the wife of Jesus will examine it with an open mind, carefully considering the possibility and giving it an honest hearing. In my earlier volume, *The Woman with the Alabaster Jar*, I presented extensive circumstantial evidence for the existence of the lost Bride of Jesus: the Mary whose epithet was "the Magdalene." She was the sister of Martha and Lazarus of Bethany. This present book describes my personal search for this forgotten Beloved and provides direct evidence of the *hieros gamous* (sacred marriage) union at the heart of the Christian story.

One underlying enigma encountered during my quest—perhaps the strangest one of all—was the ever-recurring image of the Black

Madonna. This archetypal feminine image keeps appearing in dreams, in art, in history, and in nearly four hundred shrines around the world, about half of which are located in the southern part of France, in the very region where the legends of Mary Magdalene's life and ministry proliferated. Almost without exception, these dark images are understood to be the mother of Jesus, holding the Divine Child on her lap.

In 1978, when pictures of the icon of Our Lady of Czestochowa, the Black Madonna for whom Pope John Paul II has such special devotion, were published worldwide, I was taken aback. She did not match my stereotyped image of the beautiful madonna based on my study of medieval religious art. I had not the vaguest inkling of the multifaceted symbolism of the dark lady—why she was black, why she seemed distraught, or why her icon bore ugly scars across her right cheek. It has taken years for her story to unfold, bringing with it an understanding of her significance in my own life and in the Christian paradigm.

In 1997 it was widely reported that Pope John Paul II was strongly considering naming Virgin Mary, the Blessed Mother, the "Co-Redemptrix" with Christ, a possibility that engendered strong opposition from many quarters. Roman Catholics have been instructed, through the centuries, to believe without question that everything we were taught in catechism class was the whole truth and nothing but the truth. The traditional understanding of the Catholic Church has been that the Virgin Mary's acceptance of her role was a prerequisite for the incarnation of Jesus: Her willingness to be the mother of Jesus preceded his role as Savior. She was the human "gate" or "portal"—the conduit—for the incarnation of Christ, but never his equal. Prominent theologians were reportedly united in opposing the pope's stating this new doctrine ex cathedra, citing the dearth of scriptural support for this exalted interpretation of Mary's role and the expressed dismay of the ecumenical community.

Tradition has long honored the mother of Jesus for her human role, always falling short of naming her an equal partner of Christ.

But in the canonical Gospels of the Christian faith, it was not the *mother* of Jesus who was his intimate counterpart, nor is it she who is prominent in the suppressed Gnostic traditions rediscovered in 1945 in the Coptic library at Nag Hammadi.[3] These significant books were concealed in jars in the Egyptian desert by a Gnostic sect in about A.D. 400 in the wake of persecutions by the official Christian Church of the Roman Empire. They were held in the dark bosom of the earth until after the end of the Second World War, when they were accidentally discovered by a Bedouin peasant.

In these suppressed Gnostic texts, it is not the Blessed Mother who is named as the constant companion and consort of Christ. It is Mary Magdalene who is called his *koinonōs*,[4] a Greek word bearing conjugal connotations. In the early days of the Church, it was this "other Mary" who was his Beloved. Perhaps we need now to address fairly the question of true partnership: Who was the "first lady" among the early Christians? And what ever happened to *her* version of the story?

It is time to determine whether another—earlier!—alternative to the Christian saga might resonate with truth and inspiration, opening our minds and hearts anew to the ongoing Word of God that seeks a dwelling place within us. This "reclaimed" version would include the neglected and forgotten feminine, setting us free at last from long centuries of male-oriented traditions and the stifling hegemony of male celibate priests for whom the highest virtue has long been proven to be obedience rather than love. The perceived misogyny of Christianity was not indigenous to the Church in its infancy and was never the teaching of Jesus. My intent is to restore the paradigm of sacred partnership that was once at the very heart of the Christian message.

Perhaps this story of my quest for the layers of truth and meaning of the Holy Grail will help others to embrace the conclusion I have found inevitable: that the sacred union of Jesus and his Bride once formed the cornerstone of Christianity. It was this cornerstone—the blueprint of the Sacred Marriage—that the later builders rejected, causing a disastrous flaw in Christian doctrine that has warped Western civilization for nearly two millennia. In reclaiming the lost Bride—the Goddess in the Gospels—we will restore a precious piece of our own psyches: the sacred feminine too long denied.

Note: Since the publication of my earlier book, *The Woman with the Alabaster Jar*, I have discovered that an important word often used in that volume has an alternative spelling that is closer to its Greek original. Because the Bible codes of the New Testament so illuminating in my search were based on the original Greek texts, I have adopted in the present work the variant spelling of *Magdalene* with a final "e." The final proof of the intimate partnership of Magdalene and Jesus has lain hidden for nearly two millennia in the *gematria* of their names.

In keeping with my desire to reclaim the neglected feminine in Christianity, I have capitalized Bride when speaking of the archetype and Church as her communal manifestation, the community of Christian believers. I have capitalized Temple when speaking of the center of religious and civic life of the Jewish community. When speaking of certain doctrines of the patriarchal establishment, I have attempted to "let go," rendering them in lower case: i.e., apostolic succession.

In an attempt to be understood by the general reader, I have written in the vernacular. While aware of the use of C.E. (Current Era) and B.C.E. (Before Current Era) among Bible scholars, I have chosen to use the more traditional B.C. and A.D. because they are universally understood by lay persons of all ages and educational backgrounds. The message in these pages is for the people. For the same reason and to avoid repetition of certain phrases, I have now and then referred to the Hebrew Bible as the Old Testament and the Greek Scriptures as the New Testament, along with the other widely recognized variants. I also occasionally refer to God with the traditional male pronoun, although I am acutely aware of the need to image the Divine as loving partners. It is my belief that "God" has the attitude of a loving grandmother, who does not care what you call her—just call!

The GODDESS in
the GOSPELS

To Our Lady

We have known you in
a thousand faces,
seen traces of your graciousness
in untold scores of places.
We have found you
in works of art,
in drops of dew,
and on a dragonfly's wing—
opalescent, gossamer,
and strong as fragile can be.

Your heartbeat pulses
through the universe,
steady and faithful,
bringing blossoms to bud,
birthing fawns and
hatching goslings—
web and hoof,
warp and woof
of your subtle tapestry.

Mirror of Divinity,
you bless creation
incarnate from your womb.

Source of our life, you live.

CHAPTER I

PILGRIM IN PROVENCE

I tell you if these keep silent, the stones will cry out.
(Luke 19:40)

Gnarled old vines bearing fragrant clusters of wisteria branched along the narrow street. For centuries pilgrims had ascended this winding way to the abbey church of the Magdalene crowning the hill at Vézelay, often crawling on their knees in penitence and petition. The romanesque basilica was imposing, with one massive square tower occupying the right front corner. Carved into the tawny sandstone above the entrance of "La Madeleine" was a relief showing Moses removing his shoes, a visual reminder to pilgrims to this site: "Take your sandals from your feet, for this is holy ground" (Exo. 3:5).

I resisted the impulse to remove my shoes, although medieval pilgrims would have done so upon entering the church, whose old stones were now, even as I listened, reverberating with the notes of the choir singing the evening service, calling me inside. I took a deep breath, savoring the moment and the soft, sweet air of the French countryside in springtime.

It was May 18, 1996, and I was on a pilgrimage to sacred sites of Mary Magdalene and shrines of the Black Madonna in France, feeling as if I should pinch myself to confirm the reality of the moment! I was in France for the first time in more than thirty years, preparing to enter one of the earliest and most important shrines of Mary Magdalene in Europe, a preeminent site of pilgrimage since the twelfth century—her basilica at Vézelay.

I glanced up again at Moses, reminding me that this was sacred ground, and entered the basilica, turning to the left toward the massive open door that was the original entrance of the church. Carved into the twelfth-century tympanum above the center door, the Christ was seated in majesty surrounded by figures of his saints. Looking more closely at the carved arch, I stared in awe at the imposing figure. I was stunned. Both arms of the enthroned Christ of the tympanum were outstretched in blessing, but—appallingly—his left hand was missing!

The basilica of La Madeleine was begun in 1096 in this picturesque village in the geographical heart of France. At that early date Vézelay was the fourth most popular of all sites of Christian pilgrimage, attesting to the enormous importance of Mary Magdalene at the time, based on legends that she and her family had fled to Gaul as refugees before the Gospels were even written. In 1146, fifty years after the cornerstone had been laid, Saint Bernard of Clairvaux launched the Second Crusade from the steps of this preeminent church of the Magdalene, calling his countrymen to arms for the liberation of Jerusalem.

The tympanum above the entrance at La Madeleine was desecrated during one of the many wars that plagued France for centuries, probably by an eighteenth-century revolutionary, but it is not the date of the mutilation of Jesus Christ that is important. The impact of the desecrated arch lies in the fact that in the preeminent medieval shrine of the Magdalene in Europe, it is Christ's *left hand* that is missing.

Knowing that medieval symbolic language identifies the *left* hand with the feminine (as in heraldry, where the left half of a shield bore the coat of arms of the maternal line), it seemed uncannily prophetic to me that in this basilica dedicated to Mary Magdalene—of all the hundreds of churches in France!—Christ should be maimed in this particular way, his left hand chopped off at the wrist, as if to show irrevocably that he is just not whole without *her!* Jesus once assured the Pharisees that if his disciples remained silent, the very stones would cry out. I would maintain that the stones at Vézelay are eloquent!

A special altar to the Magdalene occupies a large alcove on the right side of her basilica, where numerous votive candles keep their vigil before her. Here she stands serene, gracefully gowned, long hair flowing beneath her veil, arms extended, hands clasped, holding the chalice slightly tilted against her lower body. It is a chalice she holds cradled against her body, not the traditional alabaster jar. At Vézelay, Magdalene clasps the Holy Grail in a pose evocative of a mother cherishing her unborn child. She wears an enigmatic smile and is the very incarnation of tenderness and grace.

On this day of my pilgrimage to Vézelay, I wanted to remain before the statue of Magdalene, basking in her gentle presence and reflecting on her role as the incarnation of the "Hagia Sophia" of the Greeks—"Holy Wisdom." She was the archetypal Sister-Bride and Beloved of Jesus, his "mirror" image in the feminine. Her sweet smile caught at my heart—I wanted to know her better, to spend more time in her presence.

However, the afternoon schedule of our pilgrimage required that I continue my journey, so I finally tore myself away from the lovely statue of Magdalene cradling the Grail and continued down a short, narrow staircase into the crypt carved from the rock foun-dation of the basilica. Votive candles caused flickering shadows on the low ceiling between the arches in the crypt, where relics of Mary Magdalene were kept in a rectangular glass replica of the Ark of the Covenant. Nearby stood a vase of crimson roses—red for the passionate one who, at least for the earliest generations of Christians, embodied *ekklesia*—"the Church" in Greek—the Bride whom Christ loved so much he gave his life for her. They under-stood that Mary Magdalene was the human form of the archetypal Beloved of Christ.

On this day, May 18, 1996, the pope's birthday, I knelt in the crypt of "La Madeleine" to pray for Pope John Paul II and the patri-archs of the Church of Rome. *Do they know that the carving of the Christ in the tympanum of Magdalene's shrine at Vézelay is missing its left hand?* I wondered. *Have they understood the deeper meaning of this desecration? Do they realize that the disfigurement of the Christ at Vézelay echoes the loss of the Beloved and the consequent neglect and devaluation of Woman and all the children through nearly two millennia of Christianity? If they knew, would they care?* These thoughts haunted me as I prayed for the hierarchy of the Roman Catholic Church and especially for the pope on his birthday, feeling the significant coincidence of my pilgrimage to "La Madeleine" on this particular date.

It is a widely circulated fact that an eclipse of the sun occurred on the date of Pope John Paul II's birth, May 18, 1920. A potent prophecy lies inherent in synchronicity. An "eclipse of the sun" is a misnomer for the celestial event it attempts to describe, seeming to suggest that the sun is somehow "closed out." However, the sun is not really lost during an eclipse. It is still in its assigned place in the sky, but it is brought into a visible *conjunction* with its Sister-Bride, the moon. An eclipse is a symbol in the heavens—however brief!—for the "Sacred Marriage." *Does the Polish pope understand the momentous significance of this symbol of the intimate partnership of the masculine and feminine energies, the* hieros gamos *in the heavens?* I wondered. *Perhaps it is this* conjunctio *of the celestial bodies on the day of his birth that helps him to intuit the need to restore the feminine to a place of honor in the Christian paradigm,* I speculated.

In the twelfth century, an Irish monk named Malachy O'Morgair, the bishop of Connor, is credited with having written a now-famous prophecy applying an epithetical verse to each pope elected in future centuries. At the time, there were 112 verses; each applied to a future pontificate, and, in hindsight, each has been amazingly appropriate.

The verse from Saint Malachy's prophecy that corresponds to the pontificate of Pope John Paul II is *"de laboris solis"*—translated from Latin as "concerning the eclipse of the sun." This prophetic epithet has been the subject of intense scrutiny over the past twenty years, causing speculation and debate in various quarters. I am convinced that the verse refers to the rising of the sacred feminine to true partnership with the masculine, symbolized in the conjunction of the moon and sun, that has occurred during the years of this pope's pontificate.

For it is to Pope John Paul II that we owe the recent explosion of interest in the Black Madonna, having brought media attention to her image because of his devotion to the dark Lady of Czestochowa, clearly the image of the Mother Mary holding the Divine Child on her lap. Our Lady in her many icons around the world echoes the neolithic "Triple Goddess"—the sacred feminine.

As I knelt in the crypt at Vézelay, I remembered something else: In the ancient Hebrew Song of Songs included in the Scriptures, it is not the *mother* who is dark, "swarthy," and sunburned from her labor in her brothers' vineyard; it is—very explicitly—the bride! And in those same Hebrew Scriptures, it is not as archetypal Mother that the Holy Sophia is embraced, but, again, as Bride. The archetypal partner of the sacrificed Bridegroom/King of Middle Eastern myth is almost ubiquitously identified as his Sister-Bride.

Early Christian renderings of the Virgin and her child were modeled on the far more ancient images of the Egyptian goddess Isis, the Sister-Bride of Osiris, holding the sacred child Horus, god of light, on her lap. Ritual poetry from the cult of Isis and Osiris parallels the Song of Songs, in some places word for word.[1] Both lunar and Earth goddesses of the ancient world were often rendered dark to represent the feminine principle in juxtaposition to the solar/masculine, a dualism common in the early civilizations of the Mediterranean. Numerous goddesses were rendered black: Inanna, Isis, Cybele, and Artemis, to name only a few.

For the earliest Christians, the goddess in the Gospels was Mary Magdalene, whose epithet meant "elevated" or "watchtower/stronghold." As the number codes of the New Testament prove, they honored her as the partner of Christ, a fact we will examine at length in later chapters. These number codes or gematria have been hidden in the Greek texts of canonical Scripture ever since the Gospels were written but have until recently been ignored by exegetes and scholars of the New Testament.

For example, on a trip to the Rocky Mountain Book Fair in

Denver in 1994 I happened to encounter a scholar who had served on the Jesus Seminar, the panel of Scripture scholars who voted on whether the words of Jesus quoted in the canonical Gospels were actually spoken by him. I asked the scholar whether the panel had considered the gematria of the phrases in question, and he replied that they knew that the gematria was there, but they did not know how to deal with it, so they decided not to consider it. I was appalled. The panel of experts had a significant tool for interpreting Scripture from the perspective of the original authors, and they chose to disregard it!

After peaking in the twelfth century, the unique importance of the Magdalene in Western Europe was gradually downgraded from around the mid-thirteenth century—a date that corresponds rather dramatically with the Albigensian crusade against the Cathars and the adherents of the "Church of Love." I discussed this subject at some length in *The Woman with the Alabaster Jar.*[2] The rise of the Inquisition in the thirteenth century was especially virulent in southern France in response to several Gospel-oriented versions of Christianity, popular heretical sects that severely threatened the hegemony of the Church of Rome. With collaboration from the French king, the pope mounted a crusade against the Albigensian heretics, a bloody war of devastation that lasted for a generation, wiping out whole towns and destroying the cultural flowering of the region known as the Languedoc.

During this same era, beautiful and important epithets that once belonged to the Magdalene were shifted to the Blessed Virgin Mary and churches built to "Our Lady" ostensibly honored the mother of Jesus as the preeminent bearer of the archetypal feminine—"alone of all her sex."[3] Statues and effigies of the Virgin proliferated, most often with her child on her lap, reminiscent of the Egyptian statues of Isis and Horus. After the mid-thirteenth century, the "voice of the Bride" was effectively silenced, although it is whispered that the masons of Europe kept the true faith and built its symbols into the very stones of their Gothic cathedrals.

I had heard these persistent rumors and pondered their meaning for years. Curious to see if I could unravel the secrets of the stones, I had returned to Europe to sacred sites I had not visited for more than thirty years since traveling there as a graduate student in the summer of 1963.

What was this true faith recorded in stone? I groped with this question as I left La Madeleine that day, walking down the hill in a gentle rain. *What did the medieval stonemasons know that we have forgotten?* I asked myself these same questions often as I continued on my pilgrimage to famous shrines of the Virgin Mary—Rocamadour, Clermont-Ferrand, Montserrat, Lourdes, and Chartres—and visited sites where Magdalene is highly honored—Vézelay, Marseilles, and Les Saintes-Maries-de-la-Mer. I wanted to learn the truth hidden in their stones.

CHAPTER 11

BOUND ON EARTH

I will give you the keys of the kingdom of heaven, and whatever you shall bind on earth shall be bound in heaven. (Matt. 16:19)

A week had passed since my visit to Magdalene's basilica at Vézelay. I had climbed the steep path to the summit crowned by the Cathar stronghold at Montsegur. And I had stood in the sea with the gypsies at Les Saintes-Maries-de-la-Mer, celebrating the arrival of the "three Marys" and their friends from Jerusalem, bringing with them the Holy Grail. I had accompanied the colorful throng parading through the streets behind the statue of Saint Sarah "the Egyptian" escorted by gypsy men in costume mounted on white horses, all of us shouting in unison: "*Vive Saintes Marias, vive Sainte Sara!*"

Now the itinerary of the pilgrimage had brought me on the Feast of Pentecost to Saint Victor's abbey church perched on a plaza high above the harbor in the old part of Marseilles. The day was flawless, the blue of the Mediterranean sparkling under an azure sky, colorful boats dancing in the sunlight in the marina below.

For a long time before entering the imposing structure, I stood in awed silence in front of the church, built on the site of a sixth-century abbey that housed a community of both male and female clergy. It still shelters catacombs of great antiquity where the legacy of Lazarus and Magdalene, who brought the Good News to Gaul, was celebrated. The door of the church is framed by two massive square towers, more reminiscent of a citadel than of a church.

I smiled to myself, noticing how closely the facade of Saint Victor's resembled the castle insignia of the U.S. Army Corps of Engineers, my husband's branch of military service for thirty years—and his father's before him. Military tradition runs in both of our families for generations. We have a red banner with a white castle in our living room, reminding us of my husband's distinguished career as an officer in the Corps of Engineers. I have spent my entire married life under its aegis.

For a moment I paused to reflect on the long journey that had brought me here: on my childhood as an army brat with four brothers, moving from post to post on my father's military orders, and on the three wonderful years we lived in Germany during my mid-teens. I had become infatuated with medieval history and had later majored in comparative literature, with a minor in history and a concentration in medieval studies: medieval literature, medieval philosophy, and medieval art.

In 1963 I had returned to Germany on a Fulbright student fellowship and had continued my studies at the Christian Albrechts Universität in Kiel. The following year when I returned to Maryland University, I taught German and completed my master's degree, then embarked on doctoral studies in German language and linguistics, which I never completed, opting in 1968 for marriage to Ted, who had just returned from Vietnam and was headed for graduate school in North Carolina. The years since had been a long, often strenuous journey, my husband's thirty-year career as an army officer requiring frequent military moves with our growing family of five children.

Reminiscing in the plaza before Saint Victor's, I reflected on my orthodox Roman Catholic upbringing and on my unexpected awakening to the flawed doctrines of Christianity concerning the feminine. I reflected on my passionate quest for the meaning of the Grail and the Black Madonna that had brought me to this abbey, now drenched in brilliant sunshine on this Pentecost morning. What an incredible path I had followed to arrive at this moment! What further revelations were still awaiting me on my journey?

Saint Victor's was not unique among churches along the

Mediterranean coast of France, I had learned. During the week of my pilgrimage in Provence I had discovered that many of the oldest churches in France do not have traditional spiked steeples. In fact, they typically look more like fortresses than churches. They were built with massive walls to protect people from the raids of pirates and Moors that swept their coastal areas.

The words of Martin Luther's hymn come to mind when one sees these ancient walls: "A mighty fortress is our God, a bulwark never failing." The Church of Our Lady of the Sea in Les Saintes-Maries-de-la-Mer is another such fortress-church, built for security. Many of the oldest churches had a single square tower, often equipped with a bell, which was rung for alarm as well as to call the faithful to Sunday mass.[*]

I knew from my research in earliest Christianity that it was Magdalene whose epithet was derived from "Magdala," a Hebrew word meaning "watchtower" or "stronghold." It was she who was the original model for the Church, the community that Christ loved as eternal Bridegroom. Her name and her presence seemed to be built into the very walls of the churches of France. And here I was now, visiting the Mediterranean Coast, walking where she once had walked, retracing her footsteps. For me, Provence is holy ground.

All the bells in Marseilles were ringing as I entered the church of Saint Victor and found myself face to face with *Notre Dame de la Confessione,* "Our Lady of the Witness," one of the most famous black madonnas in France. Her glistening black effigy had been brought up from her accustomed niche in the crypt to celebrate the official birthday of Christianity on Pentecost. She was dressed in green, symbol of hope and fertility, and was holding her child in her arms. Surprisingly, she wore a large silver brooch in the shape of the fleur-de-lis, the emblem of the royal Merovingian kings of France during the fifth through the seventh centuries—the royal dynasty rumored to have been descended from the union of Christ and Mary Magdalene.[1] The symbol is now commonly identified with France. Our Lady was definitely French. And she was smiling.

I stood now before her glistening countenance, remembering

details of her preeminent folk festival on February second, Candlemas, when men with torches bear her statue up the staircase out from her accustomed niche in the crypt and carry her through the streets of Marseilles. Little boat-shaped cookies called *navettes* are baked to celebrate the arrival of the early Christians on this feast of the Black Madonna, a holy day corresponding to Imbolc and the feast of the Celtic Saint Bridget, festivals of earth-quickening and bringing in the spring. These little cookies, about five inches in length, have a split down the center that forms the interior of the boat in the shape of a Vesica Piscis, a shape long identified with the fertility of the Earth goddess. The *navettes* are also reminiscent of the "barque of Isis" in which the bereaved goddess sailed to distant shores in search of her mutilated spouse, Osiris, and it is possibly that they were once baked in her honor, since she, too, was historically celebrated in this region of Roman Gaul. The myths of Isis and Mary Magdalene have much in common, I realized. Both were widows and each bore a child after the death of her sacrificed Bridegroom.

I found it particularly fascinating during my travels in Europe to note how Christian myths, legends, rituals, and even buildings had been superimposed on those of pre-Christian inhabitants of the area, as in the case of these rites of the Black Madonna still practiced in Marseilles.

Today however was not a feast of Our Lady. Today the universal Church celebrated the tongues of fire that descended upon the apostles on the first Pentecost, denoting the infusion of the Holy Spirit that had emboldened them to set out to preach the Gospels to all nations. It was the birthday of the official Church. Later, according to legend, Magdalene and Lazarus and their sister Martha brought the Good News to Gaul, to this very city.

Descending an impressive wide staircase, I entered the crypt, where the catacombs of early Christians lined the walls. Rounding a corner, I stopped suddenly, stunned at the sight of a relief tableau carved into the stone wall facing me. In the background, Christ hung on the cross, flanked by the two thieves crucified with him. In the foreground, Magdalene was kneeling, obviously distraught, her long unbound hair streaming, her arms clasping a large rock. The effect was startling: Because of the size and rounded contour of the rock, she looked nine months pregnant!

Perhaps this was another case of "eloquent stones" trying to call out to us, I thought, staring in disbelief at the carved scene in the wall. The relief tableau is probably from the sixteenth or seventeenth century, but it occurs in the crypt of one of the oldest Christian churches in France, a crypt that contains catacombs of an early Christian community. The catacombs allegedly housed a cult of devotees of Lazarus and Magdalene in the city where these saints are said to have sought refuge from the persecutions in Jerusalem, probably those of Saul/Paul referred to in the New Testament Book of Acts. Here in the vicinity they had reportedly lived out the remainder of their lives.

Pondering the "rock" in Mary Magdalene's arms, I remembered the "Grail" in the "Parzival" of the thirteenth-century German poet Wolfram von Eschenbach, where it is called the *"lapis exillis." Could this carving be an oblique reference to the "rock in exile?"* I wondered.

Obviously, it is not "Peter's rock" that Magdalene holds. She is the "bearer" of a very different tradition, an alternative Christianity founded on the Gospels. Perhaps this rock she clasps represents this other church—the church in exile, the Church of the Holy Grail.[2] Legends affirm that Magdalene was the vessel of the *sangraal,* the royal bloodline of Israel—of King David and of Christ. She is claimed to be the ancestor of the French royal bloodline through the Merovingians.

This incredible relief carving of Magdalene is situated just feet away from the shrine of the Black Madonna, *Notre Dame de la Confessione,* honored for her role in bringing the gospel to France. *But which Mary actually carried the gospel to France?* I wondered. *Or was it both?* French legends hold that "three Marys" came to France—an echo of the Triple Goddess of the ancient world and of the three Marys mentioned in the Gnostic "Gospel of Philip" discovered in the Nag Hammadi library, which calls them constant companions of Christ: "His sister and his mother and his companion were each a Mary."[3]

Elated with the message of the stones confirming my belief that Magdalene had indeed been the mother of a child of Jesus, I climbed the stairs to hear the mass for Pentecost Sunday with the assembled French congregation. I was gradually drawn into the words of the Gospel reading: ". . . whatsoever you shall bind on earth, shall be bound in heaven."

What they had bound on earth was held bound. Yes. It was true. Bondage was a good word for it. Ancient taboos about women paraded across the meadow of my mind—along with feelings of repression, of inferiority, of lacking clout, of being relegated to menial tasks, of being muzzled. I had grown up with four brothers in a family where military service was an honored tradition. I now vividly recalled crying myself to sleep on the day when I had discovered that girls could not attend West Point. I had stated my wish to follow our family's tradition of attending the academy, and my brothers had laughed. I had fled to my room in tears.

Other memories flooded into my consciousness. I recalled watching the movie *Heidi* on that famous night in 1968 when it preempted the end of a nationally televised football game, and feeling the devastation of the little girl whom no one wanted—not her aunt, not her grandfather, and especially not the fans watching the televised football game, who later registered vigorous complaints with the network. I thought of the horror I felt when I first read of England's Henry VIII and the wives he divorced or beheaded because they were barren or had borne a daughter, and I thought of women through the centuries who have apologized to their husbands for having failed to give them a son.

I thought of all the diapers, dishes, and toilet bowls I had scrubbed, of all the "command performances" I had attended as a dutiful military wife, and then I thought of the widely circulated statistic that two-third of the manpower hours worldwide are worked by *women* for 10 percent of the remuneration. And, still seated in the pew of Saint Victor's, I remembered the look on my little daughter's face—half shock, half grief—when she asked me in 1980 whether they let women play soccer in the Olympics, and I said no. At least that much had changed in the interim years!

Now I was stifled by my built-up resentment of the establishment that did not honor or appreciate women's contributions or even their opinions—and on all the times when I have been told that my own views were irrational or irrelevant.

The words of the Gospel reading kept running through my mind: "Bound on earth, bound in heaven." I thought of the women I knew—the daughters, wives, and mothers of the Western world. The powerful gender stereotypes of the established order had not physically bound our feet, although that was the custom in China, where mothers were traditionally held responsible for binding the feet of their baby girls to keep them from becoming strong enough to run away from the men who exercised power over them.

The legend of the emperor whose wife had tried to escape by running away had caused centuries of untold misery for little girls in China, whose feet were tightly bound in the cradle to prevent them from growing—crunching and mangling the tiny bones as they tried to manifest the blueprint of their heredity. For centuries countless numbers of China's daughters cried themselves to sleep while their well-bred mothers were culturally conditioned to close their ears and harden their hearts against the pitiful wails of their girl children. Western travelers to China branded the cruel practice inhumane.

But the patriarchs of Christianity had not bound our feet with cloth bindings, I realized. The misogyny of Christian patriarchs was not so overt as that in China. They had not bound our feet—or at least, not literally! Rather, they had bound our minds, and with them, our hearts, our hopes, our very lives. Their doctrines had warped two millennia of Western civilization, preventing the liberty, justice, and equality of the Gospel message from being applied to women as well as to men, preventing the feminine principle from being honored in harmony with the masculine. Anger and resentment rose like bile within me, bitter in my mouth.

I vaguely expected to feel shock at the directions my thoughts were taking. This was not a typical Pentecost meditation; I should be ashamed of myself for harboring such thoughts! But I was recalcitrant. Years of research into the feminine and sharing insights with other women had raised my consciousness on issues of gender and power, I realized. I was aware that shame was a burden laid upon women collectively—ascribed guilt, but not for any sin we had personally committed. The story had begun in the Garden of Eden, according to the biblical account in the Book of Genesis, when Eve handed Adam the apple, and it was not over yet! Woe to those who entertained any thought perceived to be at variance with the doctrines we had been so carefully taught, doctrines like that of "original sin" promulgated by the patriarchs of the power structure, "the guardians of the walls."

Heresy is not at all a matter of what is true, but only a matter of whether a view is in agreement with the "orthodox" teachings of the "fathers"—true or false! To Peter and his priests (according to their own interpretation of their own sacred writings) had been given the absolute authority and power to define which thoughts are acceptable to God and which are not. In daring to take a different position from that of the magisterium—the teaching authority of the Roman Catholic Church—a Roman Catholic risks salvation and suffers eternal punishment! Or so we had been emphatically warned.

I am well acquainted with the stigma of heresy. This charge occasionally confronts me because I believe that Jesus Christ was married, a conviction based on material I researched for my book *The Woman with the Alabaster Jar*. Some people were shocked when the book was published in 1993. Several of my staunchest Christian friends even wrote to me, expressing their dismay at what they considered my apostasy. My own father was unhappy about the book, worried that I had "lost it."

Being a heretic is extremely uncomfortable, I have learned, a very grave matter indeed. Occasionally at lectures I give, someone in the audience scoffs at my theory because it is so clearly at variance with two thousand years of the "party line" of the established Christian churches. One Christian minister called the host of a radio talk show where I was a guest and informed me and all the listeners tuned into the program that I would go to hell for teaching such heresy. Many people, even some friends of mine, are still afraid to examine the strong evidence for the marriage of Jesus published in my book, afraid they will be tainted in some way, afraid they may jeopardize their faith.

But truth does not taint us. And faith that is not based on truth must be flawed. In the first century among the earliest Christians it was *not* heresy to believe that Jesus was married.[4] In Judaism at that time marriage was considered the only natural state for an adult male. According to precepts of Jewish law and practice derived from the Torah, young men were married before their twentieth birthdays. Only in later generations was celibacy imputed to Jesus and implied by Christian doctrine with its tradition of a male celibate clergy (which was not made mandatory until 1139). At the time of Jesus in the context of historical Judaism, the mere suggestion of his celibacy would have been heretical! Jewish people would not have followed him down the street! And yet it is claimed that the apostles followed the Jewish law in all its particulars. And Jesus himself stated that he came not to destroy the law but to fulfill it . . .

Looking around, I remembered where I was—kneeling in the midst of a Roman Catholic congregation—and as the liturgy of Pentecost continued in French, my thoughts strayed again, this time to the problems of the Catholic Church, the preeminent institution of Western civilization for two millennia. Two thousand years of privileged male hegemony has left "Peter's bark"—a common metaphor for the institutional Church founded on the primacy of the apostle Peter—shipwrecked on the high seas, unable to reach safe harbor at the threshold of the third millennium. It reminds me of the great ship *Titanic*, its side gouged open by the jagged edge of an iceberg on a night in mid-April 1912 when the moon hid her face. The fate of the famed ocean liner was a direct result of hubris—pride, even arrogance, on the part of those who built and sailed the ship, ignoring the threat of the icy seas. The fate of the *Titanic* is an interesting metaphor for Western society and the institutions of its "establishment," including the Church.

The sexual scandals that have rocked the Roman Catholic Church in recent years—and the outrageous cover-ups and denials that have accompanied them—have sprung directly from traditions that evolved from the preference for an all-male hierarchy and a celibate priesthood. Rampant, unabashed hypocrisy and lack of accountability are manifest. The hierarchical model of dominance is in deep trouble—richly deserved! For, simply put and echoing the words of the Hebrew prophets, the leaders have been shepherding *themselves* instead of the sheep! The altars are defiled and the people corrupted. What was true in the words of the Old Testament's prophets chastising the errant leaders of Israel is true even now: The corruption of the priests and rulers misleads and destroys the flock (Hos. 4:4).

But my abhorrence of the abusive double standard extends to a even deeper level. In worshiping an exclusively male image of God—a "God of power and might" glorified in liturgies and creeds of three major world religions—our institutions have entrenched a power-oriented value system that occasionally nods toward the feminine counterpart, especially if she is young and beautiful, but fails to honor her. The wisdom of the feminine, the unconscious, the body, the earth, has been "held bound" by our current institutions and customs. And we are not even aware to what great extent this is true! The subtle balance of the opposite energies has been lost for millennia, compounded in this current century with its high-technology discoveries and instant communications.

What kind of world could we live in now if the founders of Christianity had acknowledged that the sacred union of male and female, of Bride and Bridegroom, once lay at the heart of the Christian message, embodied in the intimate relationship of Jesus and Mary Magdalene? I pondered the question as the Pentecost service continued to flow around me in French. *What would the partnership mandala indigenous to Christianity have done for us if it hadn't been broken in the cradle of the new religion? What has the model of a "virgin mother" and a "celibate son" done to our collective psyche over the centuries?* . . .

For two millennia, these doctrines have robbed us of a model for relating to one another as real and equal "flesh and blood" partners.

We have not been taught to honor our bodies as sacred vessels of life, and this neglect of our own bodies has extended to our planet—our dear mother "vessel"—as well. How different our experience might have been if we had understood that sexual union is both sacred and holy! I am convinced that a model of Bride and Bridegroom, united in intimate mutuality and loving service, could have molded us into a different society—a more integrated, wholesome community—and I am convinced that reclaiming the lost model of sacred union in Christianity can help to heal us now. To reclaim this lost paradigm of wholeness and harmony, we must first restore the lost Bride of the Christian story—the Goddess in the Gospels—to her rightful place at the side of Jesus. Perhaps we should picture them holding hands.

It was my love for Christ that led me to revisit the Gospel story in search of his lost Bride. Years of research had convinced me that the celibacy of Jesus was a false doctrine and that the interpretation of the New Testament needed to be revised to include his wife. But who was this wife, and why was she not mentioned in the Gospels? I wondered. What could have happened to her?

According to Scripture, God's Messiah, the Anointed One, will give sight to the blind and cause the lame to walk; comfort the broken-hearted and proclaim liberty to captives; and set prisoners free and proclaim the day of God's favor. These messianic activities prophesied by Isaiah are recognized in the actions and miracles of Jesus in the Gospels. No mention here of bondage in heaven or on earth! The God of the Hebrew Scriptures did not wish his people to serve in bondage, but rescued them from slavery in Egypt and brought them home from captive exile in Babylon.

Based on the New Testament texts, Christians are quick to claim that Jesus was the promised Messiah of Israel, fulfilling ancient prophecies from the Scriptures, but they almost universally fail to mention the woman who anointed Jesus—the woman with the alabaster jar who knelt before him, poured her fragrant unguent over his head, and dried her tears from his feet with strands of her hair. And yet the Hebrew word *messiah* literally means "the Anointed One." And, although the details vary a little, there is only one story of an actual anointing of Jesus recorded in the canonical Gospels of the Christian faith: an anointing by a woman at a banquet in Bethany!

My research had shown me that in the ancient rites of the Near East, it was a royal bride who anointed the king. Together they embodied the Divine in a life-sustaining partnership—the *hieros gamos*. My revised interpretation of the anointing scene from the Gospels outlined in *The Woman with the Alabaster Jar* sheds new light on the dangerous fracture in Christian doctrine, providing a partnership model to transform Christianity at the threshold of the approaching third millennium.

The anointing of Jesus in the Gospels is an enactment of rites from the prevailing fertility cult of the ancient Middle East. In pouring her precious unguent of nard over the head of Jesus, the woman whom tradition has identified with "the Magdalene" ("the Great"!) performed an act identical to the marriage rite of the *hieros gamos*—the rite of the anointing of the chosen Bridegroom/King by the royal representative of the Great Goddess!

Jesus recognized and acknowledged this rite himself, in the context of his role as the sacrificed king: "She has anointed me in preparation for burial" (Mark 14:8b). Those who heard the Gospel story of the anointing at the feast in Bethany would certainly have recognized the rite as the ceremonial anointing of the Sacred King, just as they would have recognized the woman, "the woman with the alabaster jar," who came to the garden sepulcher on the third day to finish the anointing for burial and to lament her tortured Bridegroom. She found an empty tomb.

Highlights of this story recounted in the four Christian Gospels are reminiscent of myths celebrated in pagan fertility cults of the Middle East, those of Tammuz, Dumuzi, and Adonis. In the pagan rituals surrounding the ancient myths, the Goddess (the Sister-Bride) goes to the tomb in the garden to lament the death of her Bridegroom and rejoices to find him resurrected. "Love is stronger than death" is the poignant promise in the Song of Songs and similar love poetry of the Middle East celebrating these ancient rites of the Sacred Marriage.

Over a period of several years, my research had led me to examine this story from many angles. During the Middle Ages the most prevalent and popular of the so-called miracle plays were those that reenacted the anointing and the recognition scenes of the Bride and Bridegroom in the garden on that first Easter morning.[5] Artworks depicting the *Noli Me Tangere*—"Do not cling to me"—proliferated in Europe, based on the passage in John's Gospel when Mary Magdalene encountered the risen Christ in the garden and embraced him ecstatically, only to be told that she should not cling to him!

In Latin translation, the Greek verb meaning "cling to" was changed to one meaning "touch," with a subsequent shift in the sense of the passage. In medieval Latin translations of this line, Jesus said, "Do not touch me," a much harsher admonishment than that intended in the original Greek. The frequent rendering of this passage in medieval art reflects a demonstrated fascination with the theme of the abandoned Bride, the once-recognized representative of the Great Goddess from the ancient myths.

During my years of research into the Grail mystery, I had learned much about the faith of the early Christians. For the Jewish contemporaries of Jesus, the correct identity of the "Bridegroom" (the Davidic Messiah) would have been "faithful son" or "faithful servant" of Yahweh. Jesus was called the Lamb led to slaughter. He was "the shoot" of the cherished vine of Israel, "the scepter" from the root of David. He was acknowledged in the New Testament as the Lion of Judah and the Son of David. He was also called the Son of Man, prophet, priest, shepherd, king, and Messiah.[6]

If the anointing was actually Jesus' marriage rite and Mary of Bethany his wife, then important traditional beliefs of Christianity are radically affected. In this case, Jesus was not the celibate deity insisted upon by a much later Christian tradition. The "heresy" was the later implied doctrine of his celibacy, not the original model of the Sacred Marriage!

This new version of the story does not detract from the uniqueness of Jesus, but it does require a revision of the orthodox, traditional view.

It adds a flesh-and-blood dimension to Jesus that has been too long denied. This version of the Christian story presents us with a very human Jewish man, whose lineage was that of the royal dynasty of King David, and his very human Jewish wife, the two consecrated together in marriage as one flesh—the "New Adam," the "New Eve."[7]

Early exegetes of the Christian scriptures also recognized Mary Magdalene as the figure of Holy Wisdom and the Bride from the Song of Solomon.[8] In the Gnostic litany of "The Thunder Perfect Mind," a text discovered among the codices at Nag Hammadi in Egypt,[9] we find Divine Wisdom called "the honored and the scorned, the whore and the holy one"—images summed up in early traditions surrounding Mary Magdalene. Litanies and aretalogies of Isis, along with passages from Jewish wisdom literature very similar to those of "The Thunder Perfect Mind," are strongly reminiscent of the role of the Magdalene in the New Testament. Early Christians understood her archetypal role as the incarnation of the "Holy Sophia": Just as Christ embodied the Divine as the eternal Bridegroom, the Sophia was seen to be the incarnation of God's glory, the mirror of God's wisdom. The "Shekinah," the divine consort of Yahweh, enjoyed similar status among the Jewish mystics. And among the earliest generations of Christians, it was Mary Magdalene who was cast in this role as "Sister-Bride" of Christ.

The Greek goddess associated with the constellation Virgo was the fertility goddess Demeter. Popular interest in the constellations of the zodiac and the orderly precession of the equinoxes motivated the Christian patriarchs of the Hellenized Roman Empire to present a *hieros gamos* for the emerging Christian consciousness based on the location of the constellation Virgo located on the axis of Pisces.[10] Together, Virgo and Pisces were aligned as "partners" to govern the new age dawning at the exact moment in history when the Christian religion was being formulated.

In the decades that followed the crucifixion of Jesus, perhaps because the actual bride of Jesus was lost to the story, the attributes of "Virgo"—the Goddess counterpart of Jesus—were assigned exclusively to the Virgin Mary, and doctrines of her elevated status and perpetual virginity evolved and were officially stated at church councils assembled in the years A.D. 451, 553, and 649.[11] Inherent in the concretized doctrines of the Virgin Birth was the denial of the siblings of Jesus, in direct contradiction of numerous scriptural references to his brothers and sisters, passages that use the Greek word *adelphi*, meaning "from the same womb."

In the wake of doctrines extolling the status of the Virgin Mother, Mary Magdalene (so like prototype of the Bride found in the Song of Songs!) was stripped of her mantle of honor. But, as we shall see in the final chapters of this book, the epithets of Magdalene and her unique *gematria*, the number codes of the New Testament derived from the ancient canon of sacred geometry, clearly indicate that she was originally understood to have been the true partner of the Christ.

The unique role of Mary Magdalene was perhaps, at least initially, deliberately obscured because the truth was so dangerous to her and her offspring, who might have been harmed because of their relationship to Jesus. In later centuries it was misunderstood, downgraded, misinterpreted, and finally denied altogether in the Christian story. Her importance in the original community of Christians needs to be reexamined in light of the Gospel account of the anointing at the banquet at Bethany.

Every step of my pilgrimage in Provence confirmed my growing conviction that the Sacred Feminine incarnate in Mary Magdalene is a great gift for the Church, too long denied. And with each step, I became more convinced of the role I must play in the effort to restore the Goddess to Christianity.

In releasing Magdalene from bondage and enthroning her with Christ in a celestial model of intimate partnership, we will restore a healing balance "on earth as it is in heaven." And in restoring this blessing of partnership, each individual will reclaim a precious piece of human nature. We will teach one another to honor the body with its deep intuitive wisdom and the planet Earth as the source of life. We will learn to laugh again, and to appreciate beauty. We will learn

to honor and appreciate feminine attributes of gentleness and relat-
edness, feminine values of intuition and inspiration, and feminine
roles of nurturing alongside and in harmony with prevailing masculine values.

The legend of the Holy Grail promises that when the sacred vessel is found, the wasteland will be healed. My spiritual journey over
these years has convinced me that the lost Grail is a symbol for the
sacred feminine incarnate in the lost Bride (and in each of us!). She
has been gone too long and has been sorely missed, in my own
"sun/son"-oriented life and in the world! In restoring Magdalene to
her original place of honor, we will reclaim the long-devalued feminine at all levels: in our individual hearts, our homes, our entire civilization.

The notes of the last hymn died away, and the crowd of wor-
shipers began to disperse. I wandered back down into the crypt for
one last look at Mary Magdalene clasping the rock. There in the
crypt, just a few yards from Magdalene's image on the wall, a young
family was celebrating the baptism of an infant daughter dressed in a
white lace gown. A lump rose in my throat as I thought of the baby
I believe was born after the crucifixion, the baby who never saw her
father's loving smile—Magdalene's daughter. Like the stones at
Vézelay, those at Saint Victor's cry aloud!

THE DARK BRIDE

I am black—but beautiful . . . Do not stare at me because I am swarthy, because the sun has burned me . . . (Cant. 1:6).

Twas not until I climbed the rock ruins of the Cathar fortresses in southern France that I finally recognized my Templar connections. No wonder the sun-soaked stones of the citadels felt so familiar! They were part of my own personal myth. I was born at West Point, an aerie high on the west bank overlooking the Hudson River about fifty miles north of New York City. It is a walled fortress, a stronghold hewn from igneous rock. Seen from the river, its granite silhouette is as formidable as that of any medieval prototype.

Standing on the high battlements of the medieval fortress at Peyrepertuse, I remembered the generations of men in my family who spent their lives serving in the armed forces of the United States, protecting the democratic values of equality, freedom, and justice for all—values nurtured by the Gospels of Christianity—and suddenly I felt deeply connected to the Templar and Crusader families of medieval Languedoc. It was a startling realization. In some way perhaps I had partaken of their myth and was strangely linked to these French families—the custodians of the Grail secret.

Memories of my youth climbing the rocks and hiking in the woods around West Point came to me, along with memories from the mid–seventies when my husband was stationed there and we showed our children the old fortresses and redoubts in the hills.

In the summer of 1974, when Ted's military orders assigned him to teach engineering courses at the military academy, we moved our family from Fort Leavenworth, Kansas, to West Point. It was "home coming," since both of us had been born there while our fathers served on the faculty at the academy. Our military forebears had been close friends for three generations, and both our fathers had competed on the United States' Olympic team as military pentath-letes in the 1936 Games in Berlin. My parents have a picture of Ted and me building a sand castle together on a beach in Hawaii when we were children.

We drove down the familiar streets of the academy on the Hudson, revisiting the scenes of our youth and of our courtship while Ted was a cadet. It all seemed so familiar—the gray granite walls of the academic buildings and the grand old oak trees, the parade field dominated by the massive square tower of the Cadet Chapel on the hill, the chapel where my maternal grandparents had been married in 1916.

My maternal grandfather, Herman Beukema, had been a profes-sor of social sciences at the military academy for more than twenty years, and I had spent numerous summers visiting my grandparents in their three-story duplex quarters on Washington Road—"Professors' Row"—with its fantastic view up the Hudson River toward Newburgh. I remembered the bearded irises that my Dutch grandfa-ther cultivated in profusion in his garden, and the old weeping wil-low tree that grew next to the flagstone patio near the stone wall that ran along the back of the garden in those days. I used to climb up to the top of the wall and sit there, dangling my legs over the edge.

The shady patio was my favorite place when I was small—truly sacred ground—because it was there that my parents had been mar-ried. I had heard the story many times and had seen home movies of this most romantic garden wedding. I used to spend hours sitting on the flagstones where this fairy-tale event had taken place in my grandparents' garden. My grandfather had escorted my mother down the path in the center of the garden under the three rose trellises, while my father had passed under the grape arbor on the right side of the garden on his way to the patio in the far corner. It had been sprinkling all day, but the sun broke through the clouds just in time for the wedding. I have always known there was a rainbow, though no one ever mentioned it to me.

Five years later, I was brought home as a newborn baby to my own father's quarters, a big old red brick house located high on the hill near the Roman Catholic chapel, less than a city block from my grandparents' house. The pastor, Father Moore, lived in the rectory and was our neighbor. He baptized me in the chapel on October 4, 1942. I did not know until years later when I stumbled across my baptismal certificate that I was baptized on the feast day of Saint Francis of Assisi, my favorite male saint. It is rumored that his Provençal mother was a Cathar and that she profoundly influenced his unique spirituality. I know he influenced mine!

I was my mother's third child in four years, so my grandmother, in a spontaneous act of generosity, sent her cook, Rosa, up the hill to help my mother with her strenuous household. Soft, dark Rosa always smelled of lavender and she cuddled and cradled me when I was tiny, whenever my mother was too busy.

Rosa had no children of her own, so she lavished a great deal of love and attention on my brothers and me during those years we spent at West Point and later when we would return to visit my grandparents. Year after year, Rosa could be found in the back corner of her aromatic kitchen, creating savory stews, bread, or muffins by some secret alchemy . She always poured real cream on our oatmeal when we were small. She was the very embodiment of gracious bounty—like the dark Madonna herself!

The image of the Black Madonna played an incredibly important role in my own gradual awakening to the fatal flaw in the doctrines of Christianity. In 1977 when I was pregnant with my fourth child, a friend sent me a verse from the Hebrew Song of Songs (also known as the Canticle of Canticles and the Song of Solomon). The verse mentioned the blackness of the Bride, swarthy and sunburned from her work in her brothers' vineyards.

I had seen the verse before, but its significance had never struck me. In her letter, my friend had said that I reminded her of the dark Bride because I was so busy tending my family that I had no time for myself. This was true, I realized, not only of me, but of virtually every young mother on the planet, and it struck me as a profound metaphor for the condition of women in general, working in their "brothers' vineyards."

The dark Bride in the Song of Solomon is the scriptural prototype of the Black Madonna found in so many European shrines, and I can remember the painful shock I felt later that year when I first viewed the scarred countenance of the dark Lady of Czestochowa. According to traditional interpretation by first Jewish and then Christian theologians, the dark and swarthy Beloved in the Canticle is a metaphor for the archetypal Bride—*"ekklesia"*—the community of the faithful awaiting the touch of the eternal Bridegroom. And yet the Madonna of Czestochowa appeared shockingly wounded, scarred, almost distraught.

The story of Cinderella provides a secular version of the same theme from the Canticle. She is the servant girl, burned out from meeting the capricious demands of her shrewish stepmother and stepsisters. She, too, is black, sooty faced from the hearth she faithfully tends. In the German story, she is called "Aschenputl." In all versions of the Cinderella story, the blackness of the Bride symbolizes willing service and self-renunciation, echoing the theme of the Canticle.

Even in this devalued condition, swarthy from her labors in the sun, the Bride in the Song of Songs is chosen by the Bridegroom, who calls her "beloved" and "dove" and "little sister." Exegetes of Scripture recognize her also as the figure of Wisdom, the bride whom Solomon sought above all others: the Holy Spirit, or "Hagia Sophia." She is described as a "garden fountain" and a "garden enclosed." A glance at the wisdom literature in Scripture shows us that Wisdom is personified as a woman, walking the streets, trying to interest people in her wares, but few are interested. She is perennially ignored, neglected, and devalued while people greedily pursue materialism, power, and dominion.

Rather than identifying the image of the Black Madonna exclusively with the mother of Jesus, I have always identified her with the dark Bride in this Hebrew Song of Songs, the Canticle of Canticles. Lore and legends about the comely Bride proliferated through the years of my quest, and I garnered them carefully and gathered them in. As I collected the images and stories, a new seed of love and compassion for the feminine and for all feminine creatures began to take root in my soul. However, this was not to the exclusion of my long-ingrained honor and love for masculine values of reason and order and the males in my life—father, brothers, husband, and sons—but in partnership with them.

Years ago I read a best-selling romantic novel written by Thomas Costain called *The Black Rose*. As a teenager, it was my favorite book, read and reread, probably because of my delight at the truly miraculous reunion of the hero and heroine at the end. At the time, I had never heard of a black madonna. The only statues of the Virgin Mary I had ever seen were white. And I did not consciously associate the heroine of the novel with my childhood nurse, Rosa. I knew nothing about psychology, nothing about personal myths or the unconscious associations that often serve as guides, pressing us forward along the way toward enlightenment and transformation.

I did not realize that I was predisposed from childhood to love this novel, because already—all my life—I had loved Rosa. The memory of warm, dark Rosa lingers still—her fragrant presence the shade of *café au lait*, exotic gold hoops in her ears. How could I have guessed that I would stumble onto this romantic story and be moved to embark on a search for the "Black Rose," to discover who she really is and why she was called "Beloved" and "Sister-Bride."

In Costain's novel, the woman called the "Black Rose" was named Miriam. The story was adapted from a legend told of the parents of Saint Thomas à Becket, the English hero-saint assassinated by agents of the ruthless Plantagenet King Henry II. Becket's mother was reportedly a Middle Eastern princess who became separated from her English Crusader husband and searched for him across the entire continent of Europe.

Costain's similar story of Walter and Miriam unfolds in the thirteenth century, and the heroine traveled all the way from China,
first carrying their baby, later holding the child by the hand. It took
her several years to make the difficult and dangerous journey, but
somehow she and the child survived all the hardships and obstacles
placed in their path. She knew only two words in the English language: "Walter" and "London." And yet she found him. Beautiful,
dark Miriam was determined to find her Walter. She was sick and
starving, even delirious, when she finally reached England. It
seemed a miracle at the end of the novel when Walter at last was
told of the dark foreigner wandering in the streets of London calling
his name.

I now find it interesting that the film version of *The Black Rose*
leaves out the details Costain included of Miriam's dangerous journey, concentrating instead on the story of Walter's triumphant return
to England with artifacts and stories of his journey to Cathay, as if
only his story were of any interest or value. The woman's distressing
and painful story was not considered important to the filmmakers in
the 1950s.

But the stories of Miriam and Magdalene are so very similar: the
journey through the centuries has been long and difficult, the out-
come often hanging by a thread. The story of the risen Christ has
been told and retold, but the story of the Magdalene has been hidden. Despite the obstacles in her path, this "other Mary" has been
seeking to be reunited with her Beloved throughout the two millennia since the Gospels were written. It is time to restore her to her
rightful place of honor at the side of Jesus.

Because my antennae have been focused on the image of the
"black" Bride, I have gleaned associations from myriad sources. Saint
Bernard of Clairvaux in the twelfth century gave sermons on the
Canticle calling Mary of Bethany—the sister of Martha and
Lazarus—the prototype of the "Bride" because she sat at the feet of
Jesus drinking in his every word and gesture.

In this interpretation, Saint Bernard was echoing the opinion of
Origen (circa 185-254) and other early Christian scholars who saw

Mary of Bethany in this light.[1] Among early Christians, she was the model for the contemplative soul. It was easy to empathize with her because like her, Christians rest at the feet of Jesus, too, drinking in his instruction from the Gospels and spending time with him in prayerful meditation.

This same Mary is the model for the contemplative orders of nuns. She represents the direct personal encounter of the soul with its eternal "spouse"—the Beloved. She is the model of mystics and of Gnostics, who "know" God through the "moist" tradition of direct experience—through intuition and inspiration—rather than by indoctrination from the "dry," legalistic tradition of the established Church, including the memorization of its rules and catechisms.

Mary Magdalene was beloved as well, I knew. Early interpreters of Christian Scriptures equated her with the dark Bride of the Canticle, too. Together she and Mary of Bethany form an amalgamation of the archetypal feminine in the writings of the early exegetes of the Gospels.[2] In Western art Magdalene is the woman with the alabaster jar who anointed Jesus with costly nard and dried her tears from his feet with her hair, and John's Gospel specifically identifies this woman as the sister of Lazarus.

For me, the woman called Magdalene has always provided the most intense example of passionate love for God in all of Scripture—the lover. The calm and sure response of the Virgin Mary to the message of the angel Gabriel was an example of total surrender to the will of God, but the other Mary was the passionate one. Luke's Gospel states this woman who anointed Jesus at the banquet was a sinner and that because she had loved much, much had been forgiven her. Or was it because so much had been forgiven her that she loved so much?

My heart holds a distant echo of the love of this other Mary for Jesus. The living Christ I have encountered in the Scriptures and in my life is the only man I have ever known who does not tolerate the double standard. His love is unconditional and has blessed my life in ways immeasurable!

How interesting that the poignant theme of the separated lovers keeps recurring in literature from all over the globe! In 1986 I saw the film *Ladyhawke*, a beautiful version of this same old story. In this film, set in the medieval town of Aquila, the evil bishop lusted after the beautiful Isabeau, but she rejected him because she loved Navarre, the captain of the guard. Enraged, the despicable prelate cursed the pair, condemning them to be forever together, yet separated.

Under the bishop's spiteful curse, Navarre becomes a wolf at night, Isabeau a hawk by day, so that they never see one another in human flesh, but switch to their respective animal roles at sunrise and sunset. Finally an old hermit is shown the only way to break the bishop's evil spell: together, the lovers must stand before the bishop during *an eclipse of the sun!*—the *"conjunctio"* in the heavens.

This incredible movie is a visual hymn of the Sacred Marriage. In light of Saint Malachy's prophecy concerning the current papacy, whose prophesied epithet *"de laboris solis"* refers to a solar eclipse, I find this beautiful film intensely insightful and prophetic of the sacred reunion occurring in our generation!

And the separation and eventual reunion of the beloveds is the same poignant story that is found also in the Song of Songs! The Bridegroom appears briefly at the lattice of the window, and the Bride catches a glimpse of him, but then he slips away. Desperately, and in vain, the Bride seeks him throughout the city.

Finally the "guardians of the walls," the official representatives of the establishment, come upon her wandering alone and dejected in the city streets. They cannot permit her to be out alone at night, so they beat her, strip her of her cloak, and send her home. Clearly these men, charged with keeping order in the city, assume she is a woman of the streets—prostitute, not bride. They did not even ask to hear her story.

Ironically, the "Miriam" who was the wife of Jesus suffered a very similar fate. Instead of helping her be reunited with her Bridegroom, the "guardians of the walls," caught up in a wave of asceticism that swept through the Roman Empire in the early centuries of Christianity, stripped her of her most honored titles and status, branding her a prostitute. And for generations to come, all her sisters and daughters—Christian women worldwide—have been subject to the controlling dictates of these same well-meaning patriarchal "guardians"—bound on earth, bound in heaven!

After agonizing separation, the lovers of the Song of Songs are at last reunited in the garden—the orchard of pomegranates. The Persian word *paradise* means "an enclosed garden," and in the Song of Songs, the Bridegroom calls her "my Sister, my Bride" and "a garden enclosed." Their reunion in the orchard of the pomegranates is paradise enough! The archetypal bridal pair of the Christian story has endured painful separation for nearly two millennia. Until they are reunited, there can be no garden!

Mary Magdalene—like the "Black Rose" in Costain's novel—has been searching for her Beloved throughout nearly twenty centuries of Christianity. Her story is told in all four canonical Gospels: She is the woman with the alabaster jar, the one with the marvelous hair. She walked hand-in-hand with Jesus as soul mate, but she was also a flesh-and-blood woman, loved by a fully human Christ, tragically lost to the Christian heritage in the tumultuous aftermath of the crucifixion.

We have suffered untold deprivation in not having recognized the Bride of Jesus and the model of union that was, according to the earliest writings of the Christian community, once at the core of the religious institution upon which Western civilization was founded. Initially, her loss may have been accidental; perhaps the friends of Jesus who were trying so hard to save her life hid her too well! I am committed to reclaiming the image of the lost Bride to all levels in the human psyche, reclaiming her attributes of gentleness, beauty, intuition, and inspiration and enshrining them in a place of honor alongside the perceived masculine values of strength, order, and reason.

At the same time, we can revise our appreciation of our bodies as sacred flesh-and-blood vessels in partnership with our minds and spirits. We can start to walk in a new wholeness, with a new understanding that many attributes are not exclusively masculine or feminine:

strength, valor, grace, and intelligence are not gender exclusive, but rather they are *human* attributes shared by the entire human family!

There are strong grounds for this return of the Bride to the Christian story. Modern research into the social practices of Judaism affirms the marriage of Jesus, as do the New Testament Scriptures themselves.[3] Biological union is now and always has been a fundamental prerequisite for life on this planet. The sacred partnership of masculine and feminine energies is found in every discipline—the harmony and balance of the opposites govern music, biology, gymnastics, physics, architecture, and everything in between! The dualism of past centuries has been superseded by a new model for society—the ancient blueprint of sacred union—the ✡ of the cosmic dance!

On a symbolic level, the repudiated Bride of Jesus is an earthly counterpart to the great queens of heaven—the goddesses Inanna, Isis, Cybele, and Venus—reflected in the image of the dark Madonna. This anciently honored Goddess image is being recognized at last, not just as the "Virgin Mary," but as *the feminine face of God*—Holy Wisdom—despised, scorned, rejected, and bound for more than two thousand years. When the beloved Miriam is at last restored to her place beside Jesus, their sacred reunion—the *hieros gamos*—will reinstate an ancient pattern for wholeness and partnership that has the power to restore balance on Earth. Together they will bind up the wounds of the little ones and heal the brokenhearted, return sight to the blind, and set the prisoners free!

Before returning to the United States, the women on our pilgrimage spent our last evening in France walking the labyrinth at Chartres Cathedral, tracing the archaic spiral in the stone floor of "Notre Dame." It was May 30, 1996, the feast day of Saint Joan of Arc. My pilgrim sisters and I danced barefoot in the darkened church that night, the arches soaring above us in the shadows and the setting sun turning the stained glass of the windows to glowing jewels.

We had followed the paths of medieval pilgrims and trod in their very footsteps, pausing to pray at the preeminent shrines of the Madonna in France and southern Spain, visits that had filled me with profound peace and joy, culminating years of research centered in the dark image of the sacred feminine, and satisfying a hunger to see her many faces. When I had written *The Woman with the Alabaster Jar*, I had understood the tragic flaw in Christianity, the denial of the sacred feminine, but I had not yet personally encountered the feminine face of the Divine.

Years have now passed, and my experience of the feminine has become deeper and more profound than ever I thought possible. It has been a remarkable journey. In the chapters that follow, I want to retrace my footsteps to the early years of my faith journey, to tell of my quest to reclaim this other face of the Divine. For clearly it was she who led me to the mystery surrounding the Holy Grail and the Goddess in the Gospels.

CHAPTER IV

THE COMMUNITY
EMMANUEL

I will give you treasures out of the darkness and riches that have been hidden away. (Isa. 45:3)

When my husband's assignment to teach engineering at the military academy moved our family to West Point in June of 1974, I learned about a close-knit group of charismatic Catholics there who met often for prayer, their worship centered around the altar and liturgy of the local Catholic church, the Chapel of the Most Holy Trinity. The members of this group had met during a "Life in the Spirit Seminar" in October 1973, a week-long charismatic renewal program. Their experience bonded them as friends and touched them profoundly, providing a catalyst for an ongoing experience of awakening. Like the woman with the alabaster jar, the members of the small community consciously poured their lives out at the feet of Christ. They called themselves "Emmanuel," a Hebrew name meaning "God with us."

When we arrived on post that summer, I soon became involved in the religious education program and women's activities in the parish at Holy Trinity, and as a result, became acquainted with the women who were members of the Emmanuel community. We gathered for prayer and pondered revelations we received about the condition of the Catholic Church, and together we prayed intensely for the purification and healing of our church and its priesthood as well as for the immediate needs of our own families and friends.

Saint Paul's first letter to Corinthians describes a Christian community and its many gifts: to one person was given a gift of tongues; to another, a gift of teaching; to yet another, a gift of interpreting tongues. The Emmanuel community was similar. We shared the timely passages we encountered in Scripture, often just opening the Bible randomly and reading from the page before us, honoring it as God's word spoken directly to us in the present moment. We also prayed for understanding of the events we experienced, searching out the meaning behind the reality. We practiced the presence of God in every detail of our lives, relying on the direct guidance of the Holy Spirit. We listened in good faith to the Word of God, and we trusted in good faith that what we heard was actually and truly God's word.

Several of the individuals in the little prayer community Emmanuel felt guided beginning in 1973, a year before I met them, to record the revelations and inspirations they received in prayer—through locutions (words spoken to the heart) or timely Scripture passages. Synchronicity—meaningful coincidence—played an important role in their gradual enlightenment, although at the time none of them knew that word. They learned to search for meaning behind timely symbols and events in their lives.

One of the first recorded teachings had to do with the proper "blueprint" for the building up of the "Body of Christ," the entire membership of the institutional Catholic Church. Jan, one of Emmanuel's original members, had a statue of Jesus, called the "Sacred Heart." When it accidentally shattered, she was devastated. Her husband helped her salvage all the tiny shards of the statue and glue them back together—just because Jan couldn't bear to part with it. When they had finished reassembling the statue, one sizable piece was still missing and could not be found. A large piece of the foundation on which the Christ figure stood had mysteriously disappeared.

The next day, when they showed the broken statue to Mary Beben, another charter member of the group, she recognized a lesson in the mystery of the lost piece, one concerning the blueprint for the Body of Christ: There was a piece missing in the current pattern— and an equivalent piece missing in each human person as a result. Mary did not at all understand what was meant by this, but she continued to record the prophecy she was receiving in an extended locution, a process similar to channeling. She and her friends were asked to learn all they could because the Church was going to be shattered and they must help rebuild it according to the right pattern. A new "Body of Christ" was trying to be born according to the true blueprint, but the old image had first to be broken, and this would be very painful for the whole Church. The missing piece of the foundation and the true blueprint trying to be manifested were a mystery Mary and her friends could not at first fathom.

When I first was shown this prophecy in early 1975, I had no idea what to think of it. But as the years passed, the profound meaning of the shattered statue and the important piece lost from the foundation of Christianity has become ever more obvious! Now in light of all I have learned about the lost Bride of Christianity, I have come to understand that *she* is the piece that has been missing and needs to be found and restored, completing the model of sacred partnership that was once at the heart of Christianity. It is this absence of the feminine that causes our brokenness and so desperately needs to be healed—as above, so below!

Another recurring theme that developed through early prophecy received by the Emmanuel community was that of people thirsting and dying in the desert because the streams of God's love and wisdom had been blocked or were badly polluted. We began to notice the festering sickness within the Catholic Church and the pain it was causing the entire world. We asked to discern clearly the cause of this brokenness—what was at its root?—and we begged to be instruments to help heal the wounds. In prophecy, especially praying with Scripture passages, we were shown the defiled altars and unworthy shepherds who "shepherded themselves instead of their sheep," the assassination of the high priest, and the plunder of the "temple treasury." Occasionally we were also given glorious promises of the new and restored temple.[1]

These prophetic revelations were carefully recorded in our journals over a period of several years, even after the members of the Emmanuel community were dispersed by military orders to other assignments. Our diaspora actually forced us to record revelations and insights we received in order to continue to share our journeys with one another.

In 1977, my husband was reassigned to the Pentagon, and we moved to a house south of Alexandria in Virginia. A few weeks later, Sue, an Emmanuel sister whose family had also recently moved to northern Virginia, called me on the telephone. She had just unpacked some boxes and had discovered that the right hand had been broken off her statue of the child Jesus known as the Infant of Prague. It was the only item she noticed that had been broken during her move, but that was not what had disturbed her. She had discovered at about the same time that the right arm was broken from the figure of Jesus on the crucifix of her personal rosary. And, adding to her uneasiness, she had just discovered that another figure of Jesus, a hand-carved crucifix that her husband had sent home from Korea, was also missing its right arm, broken in transit. *Was God trying to tell us something about his right arm?* we wondered. *What was the meaning of the right hand of God?*

Sue and I both knew that these coincidences involving the right arm of Christ were not accidental in the usual sense, since we had developed the practice over the years of interpreting the symbols and events in our lives. I told her about a novel I had once read, called *The Left Hand of God*, in which a U.S. pilot shot down in China disguised his identity by dressing in the robes of a dying priest and traveling to the town where the priest had been expected. There he ministered in the role of a priest, relying on memories of the liturgies of his Catholic childhood to avoid being detected. "Perhaps the right hand of God represents the priesthood," I suggested off the top of my head, "since God's left hand was obviously represented by the layman pilot."

When the Emmanuel community members gathered several

weeks later for a planned reunion, Sue shared with them the story of her figures of Jesus with the threefold occurrence of a broken right arm. The community confirmed our discernment that the priesthood was symbolically the "right hand of God," which had become estranged from the body and was weakened and wounded, no longer able to properly shepherd and guide the faithful flock. We felt moved to offer our lives for the restoration and healing of the priesthood of the Roman Catholic Church—the "right hand of God"—a spiritual renewal of the clergy, which seemed to us to be a prerequisite for the survival and ultimate renewal of the Church.

For each of us, the commitment was made consciously. All our prayers, joys, hopes, fears, and sufferings were laid on the altar as a sacrifice offered for this intention. Our Catholic training had taught us to "offer it up to God" and we did. At the time we had no idea of the paths we would be led to take, and looking back now after all these years, I realize that it is just as well that we made this commitment without any inkling of where it would lead us. I feel sure I would have recoiled if anyone had suggested that I would become a teacher of an alternative Gospel that included the marriage of Jesus and Mary Magdalene! And my friends would have been even more shocked than I, coming as we did from the heart of orthodoxy.

That afternoon of August 26, 1977, we recorded three prophetic Scripture readings without fully grasping their significance. The first was from Zechariah 3: Joshua, the high priest—clothed in filthy rags—needed to be purified and dressed in clean festal garments. In Ezekiel 34 we read the prophecy and chastisement of the evil shepherds who scattered the flock. And then we were given the apocalyptic vision of Daniel 9:26, the cutting down of the anointed high priest of the Jewish Temple.

We recorded these Scripture passages, pondering their meaning for us in the present moment, and remembering the prophecies we had recorded over the years regarding the defiled altars of the Church, the plunder of the temple treasury, and the murder of its high priest. How were we to understand that the high priest, presumably the pope, was dressed in filthy garments? What did this mean? We were blissfully unaware at the time of the issue of sexual misconduct among priests, but already sensed that the hierarchical model of the Church had produced a class of privileged and power-ful men who were out of touch with the needs of the people. We were still at a loss to explain the prophecies about the plundered temple and the assassination of the high priest.

Events unfolding exactly a year later provided further enlight-enment. The election of Luciano Albino, Pope John Paul I, as the successor of Pope Paul VI occurred on August 26, 1978, the first anniversary of the Emmanuel community's reunion retreat in 1977. However, his tenure was extremely short-lived. The suspicious death of the "high priest" John Paul I following a brief—and symbolic!—thirty-three day reign as pontiff shocked us profoundly. We did not know what to think of this event and were unaware for several years that rumors in Europe linked the death of the pope with his intent to investigate the Vatican bank scandal. Like Jesus, it appears that this gentle shepherd had been sacrificed—literally "cut-down" by collaborating Romans and corrupt priests.

The underlying theme of our 1977 gathering had been the restoration of the priesthood as the strong and purified "right hand of God," although at the time we did not yet fully comprehend God's "right-handedness." A few months later Mary Beben wrote us all a long letter. She had unlocked and entered the small Blessed Sacrament Chapel in her parish church in Puerto Rico, where she had moved in 1976. To her horror, the right arm had broken off the figure of Jesus nailed to the huge crucifix hanging over the altar and had fallen onto the tabernacle, which in turn had toppled from the altar to the floor, broken open, and spilled its contents of consecrat-ed communion wafers all over the floor. For Mary the message was clear: the brokenness of the "right arm"—the priesthood—was caus-ing a violent desecration of the entire Church, symbolized by the scattered eucharistic bread. We were appalled!

Just as Mary had done, each member of the Emmanuel commu-nity shared significant events with all the others, mailing copies of our letters to one another regularly. The events of our lives were recorded and submitted for discernment, continually enhancing our spiritual journey and kinship. The recorded prophecies of the Emmanuel community are not incidental to my Grail quest; they are at its very heart.

Although we were stunned by the sudden and untimely death of Albino Luciano, Pope John Paul I, in 1978, we were delighted with the surprise election of Karol Wotyla, the Polish pope. A prophetic poem written in 1848 by Julius Slowacki, a Polish poet, had described a Slavonic pope who would be "a beacon for all mankind."[2] The people of Poland had cherished their dream of a Polish pope for generations, and the election of Karol Wotyla as Pope John Paul II was the answer to the communal prayer of the oppressed nation. Of course, they were ecstatic! Surely God was with them!

The newly elected pontiff began his 1978 inaugural address by quoting the opening line of the Polish national epic of freedom fighting, a significant work called *Pan Tadeuz*, powerfully reminding his compatriots of his passionate sympathy with their cause: "When the moon rises over Czestochowa . . ."

During the summer of 1980 my husband was reassigned again, this time transplanting our family of five young children to Fort Campbell, Kentucky. Events in Europe were extremely tense during that summer, with the strong possibility of a Soviet movement of tanks into Poland causing grave concern among political and military officials in the United States. One of my husband's commanders candidly stated his opinion that United States troops would be in Eastern Europe before the end of 1980.

Several years later my friends and I learned that the Polish pope John Paul II had written a letter to the Soviet leaders in the Kremlin in 1980, stating that if they rolled their tanks into Warsaw, he would be in Poland defending the trenches with his people. I was reminded of an old quip from the Middle Ages: "How many legions has the pope?" The military power of the entire Western world might well have been there with him. And his patroness, the dark Madonna, would assuredly have been at his side as well.

By nourishing the virtues of courage, faith, and hope in the hearts of the Polish people and their pope, the Black Madonna of Czestochowa stopped the Russian tanks in Europe in 1980. Worldwide, she is a patroness of freedom fighters, and Poland in particular celebrates several historical victories that occurred on feast days of the Blessed Mother. Their faith in her aid is extraordinary.

I followed the development of the crisis in Europe with avid attention. No wonder the Solidarity movement had the courage to stare down the Communist regime in Poland—they clearly believed that God was on their side! Their faith in God's intervention was intensified in May 1981, when the pope was shot at point blank range on the feast day of Our Lady of Fatima and miraculously survived. Clearly the Holy Father was a favored son of "Our Lady"! My friends and I discussed these events in letters and on the telephone, marveling at their significance and praying earnestly for the full recovery of Pope John Paul II. What must the Communist regime have thought when they saw that he lived?

Looking back upon significant events of the years between 1978 and 1989, it seems clear to me now that the election of the Polish pope at that critical time in history was one of the main factors that conspired in the dissolution of the Soviet Empire—an important element in the "domino effect" that also opened the Berlin Wall and ended the Cold War era. The official, preselected liturgical text for the day of Karol Wotyla's 1978 inauguration was powerfully prophetic of those apocalyptic events.

I had felt at the time that the papal election of Karol Wotyla in the autumn of 1978 was an extraordinary choice, and found this view radically confirmed by the official designated reading of the Church on the day of his inauguration, taken from chapter 45 of the book of the prophet Isaiah and chosen long before anyone could have possibly known that it was to be the inauguration day of a pope. The context of this passage from the prophet Isaiah describes the role to be played by Cyrus, the new governor of Israel in 517 B.C.

In the light of these scriptural verses, our prayer community Emmanuel understood that the Old Testament figure Cyrus was a prototype of John Paul II, "the foreigner." We took special notice of the role of Cyrus in Jewish history, noticing exciting parallels with the role of the new Roman Catholic leader.

The biblical text from Isaiah 45 read on the day of Pope John Paul II's anointing is astounding in its prophetic message: "Thus says the Lord to his anointed Cyrus, whose right hand I grasp, subduing nations before him, and disarming kings, opening doors before him and leaving the gates unbarred: I will go before you and *level the mountains*; bronze doors I will shatter and *iron bars I will snap*" (emphasis mine).

Contemplating the iron bars snapping before Cyrus, the "anointed of God," we are reminded specifically of the Iron Curtain—the guarded walls and rolls of barbed wire—that turned to dust in 1989 and 1990 in the wake of the freedom movements in Eastern Europe. These freedom movements received their encouragement from the Solidarity movement in Poland, whose members' formidable strength was derived from an unshakable faith that God was with them. The attributes of the Black Madonna universally include compassion, strength, and an ability to break chains and to bring down walls. She is very often identified with the oppressed and the freedom-fighters.

In the reading for the day, Cyrus the foreigner had been anointed as the instrument of God's will *"to restore the temple,"* the focal point of Jewish worship and a symbol of their national identity and their covenant with Yahweh, their God. In the prophetic passage from Isaiah, God addresses Cyrus who was the governor following the return of the Hebrew people from their seventy years of captivity in Babylon. It was Cyrus who announced that it was time to lay the foundation of a new temple in Jerusalem. Contemplating this passage, read aloud from Roman Catholic pulpits worldwide on the inauguration day of Pope John Paul II, my friends and I understood that the new pope had been chosen for a similar role.

Of course, the temple of which we are speaking in our extended metaphor of "Cyrus, the foreigner" is not the destroyed Temple of Solomon in Jerusalem, but rather the great symbolic or "mystical" temple that crystallizes in the psyche of the human race.

Pope John Paul II has not made any official pronouncement that the new temple be built. But he has nonetheless laid the foundation for a new "mystical" temple, not as yet by decree but by bringing to our consciousness a "treasure out of the darkness" in the image of the Black Madonna—the beloved feminine—and in his reported desire to name "Mary" the Co-Redemptrix with Christ. The explosion of interest in this image and in the Divine as feminine has been remarkable in the years since his inauguration, along with dramatically increased devotion to "Mary," "Our Lady," and the many faces of "Goddess," especially her dark ones.

By any name, the gradual restoration of the feminine to a place of honor is globally manifest. While the prelates in the Vatican may have wanted to prevent the feminine from assuming a more important role of ministry in the Roman Church, Pope John Paul II *in fact* instigated the controversy about women's roles simply by focusing worldwide attention on the disturbing image of the abused and abased feminine so clearly visible in the scarred visage of the Black Madonna of Czestochowa.

The verses from Isaiah 45:3–4 that inspire hope for the future are found in the promise of God to Cyrus: "I will give you *treasures out of the darkness* and *riches that have been hidden away*, that you may know that I am the Lord . . . who calls you by name . . . I have called you by name, giving you a title, *though you knew me not*" (emphasis mine).

The synchronicity of this prophetic passage having been preselected by Roman Catholic officials months before as the assigned liturgy for the day on which Pope John Paul II happened to be inaugurated is profound. God is seen calling his "anointed" servant by name to receive hitherto unrecognized truth—"treasures out of the darkness"—and asking him to realize that even he, the consecrated leader of Roman Catholics around the globe, *does not yet know the one true God*: "I have called you by name . . . though you knew me not."

I pondered this line for a long time before realizing its profound meaning: Our present understanding of God is warped—distorted by millennia of "sun/son" orientation—and the human race does not truly "know God." And yet, in Isaiah 44, God names this same Cyrus "My shepherd who fulfills my every wish; he shall say of Jerusalem: 'Let her be rebuilt!' and of the Temple: 'Let its foundations be laid!'"

It appears that the modern-day "Cyrus," Pope John Paul II, standing on the threshold of the third millennium of Christianity, has been similarly chosen to restore the true blueprint of the mystic temple, so long repressed. The denied model is inherent in the eclipse of the sun on the day of his own birth—the *conjunctio* of the sun and moon—the celestial model of the Sacred Marriage.

In the months following the inauguration of the Polish pope, the scarred visage of Our Lady of Czestochowa began to haunt me, urging me to learn the reason for her sad plight. I ferreted out information about her icon, housed at the monastery of Jasna Gora in Czestochowa and venerated in Poland for nearly a thousand years. A medieval legend says she was painted by Saint Luke; other sources maintain that she was of Byzantine origin. Still others suggest that this image was painted in France during Merovingian times, probably in the sixth century, and taken in the early ninth century by Charlemagne's armies to the Balkan Peninsula, from whence it made its way to Poland in the dowry of a tenth-century Byzantine princess.[3] Bandits had scarred her face in a raid on the church at Jasna Gora in 1403, but more than the hideous scars, it was the look in her eyes that most disturbed me. Why did she look so anguished, as if she had never smiled? Why did she seem distraught? Who was this enigmatic dark lady? I have been pondering these questions for years.

John Paul II is clearly a "faithful son" of "Our Lady," the Black Madonna of Czestochowa. But does he fully understand her image? Surely she comprises far more than the Jewish Mary, wife of Joseph and mother of the historical Jesus. Does he recognize in her the scorned and rejected feminine face of God? Does he see reflected there the desolated mourning of the widowed, the oppressed, the abandoned, and the countless little ones who cry themselves to sleep on our planet?

Surely the pope's desire to proclaim Mary as Co-Redemptrix with Christ reflects his desire to replace the mandala of sacred partnership at the center of Christianity. But does he yet realize that the several "Marys" in the Gospel *together* reflect the sacred feminine— the ancient Triple Goddess mirrored in the masculine trinitarian doctrine articulated by the early Christian fathers? And does he realize that in raising "Mary" to the status of Co-Redemptrix, he will be raising flesh to equal partnership with spirit and proclaiming for all time the intimate union of humanity and divinity? Perhaps he does!

The Black Madonna is a mighty patroness! But do we have any inkling of the full scope of her reality? In southern France alone there are several hundred Black Madonna shrines where she is honored as the Virgin Mary with her son Jesus on her lap. But the image of the beautiful dark mother is much older and far deeper than medieval Christian interpretations and traditions reflected in these statues. The image of the dark feminine goes back to the ancient neolithic representations of Earth as the Great Mother—the eternal "vessel" or "Grail"—bringing forth all that lives in endless, ongoing cycles of creative activity. And her image is found in the ritual poetry of the Sacred Marriage redacted from the ancient fertility rites of the Near East. We have found her in the Song of Solomon, in the lines of the archetypal Bride: "I am black—but beautiful."

Like the face of Helen that "launched a thousand ships," it was the desecrated face of the Black Madonna of Czestochowa that launched my quest for the lost Grail. In researching the image of the Black Madonna and her ancient renderings in pagan myth and artifacts, I encountered the ancient lore of the Triple Goddess as well as the neglected and forgotten Bride and the cult and mythology of the Sacred Marriage. Taken together, these have become the cornerstone of my life—the ✡ partnership mandala urging me to seek balance at every level of my experience.

Looking back, it seems self-evident that the scarred and burned-out "face" of the volcano Mount Saint Helens would arrest my attention.

CHAPTER V

THE DESTROYING
MOUNTAIN

Beware, I am against you, destroying mountain . . . I will stretch forth my hand against you, roll you down over the cliffs, and make you a burnt mountain. (Jer. 51:25)

On May 18, 1980, Mount Saint Helens erupted with incredible force, spewing rock and lava over thousands of square acres, snapping the trunks of 500-year-old Douglas fir trees like matchsticks and pouring the waters of Spirit Lake down the mountainside, devastating the surrounding communities with severe mudslides, intense heat, and blowing ash. It was the pope's birthday.

Vividly I recalled the readings from Isaiah 45 on the day of John Paul II's inauguration some eighteen months before: "I will go before you and level the mountains." It is not every day that a mountain is leveled and a lake called "Spirit Lake" is poured out onto the ground! The synchronicity was too potent, the dates and geographic names too evocative to be ignored.

I had visited Spirit Lake on a fishing holiday with my husband and small son in 1973, seven years before the eruption, and I well remembered the snow-covered peak of Mount Saint Helens sweeping upward above the little lake tucked away in the mountainside. The "elegant lady" of the northwest Pacific coast had reigned snow-capped and serene, towering over the landscape near the Washington-Oregon border. Every day we had rowed a boat out into the center of the crystal-clear lake fed by glacier streams dancing and cascading over rocks in spectacular waterfalls. We had savored breathtaking views of Mount Saint Helens and have numerous photographs and film footage from that vacation preserved in our family archives.

I was appalled to read of the widespread devastation caused by the volcano. During the first eruption Spirit Lake was tipped and poured out like a gigantic pitcher down the lower slopes of the mountain. On the upper reaches of the northwest wall of the mountain, glaciers of centuries melted in a matter of seconds, while mud slides poured down the face of the mountain, scouring the terrain. Giant fir trees were ignited instantaneously; some farther away were broken off like matchsticks in the mighty blast. The devastation was awesome.

Then, exactly one week later, on the evening of May 25, 1980, I was fixing supper in my kitchen when a radio newscast announcer mentioned that Mount Saint Helens had erupted again, for the second Sunday in a row. My attention was immediately riveted on this event 3000 miles away.

In spring of 1979, about a year before the eruptions of Mount Saint Helens, Ron, one of the original Emmanuel community members who was now an ordained priest, had loaned me the thesis of a friend of his, a doctoral candidate at Fordham University in New York City. The subject of the thesis was the uncanny coincidence or "synchronicity" of significant dates in history with the liturgical calendar and with the official Church readings assigned for those dates. As an example, the cited fact that Abraham Lincoln was assassinated on Good Friday speaks volumes. Abraham Lincoln has always been one of my personal heroes, but I had never known that he was cut down on Good Friday! The parallels to another "savior" were too close to be casually ignored.

Soon after reading the doctoral dissertation, I had stumbled upon a line in Ezekiel 24 that says "record this date" and had begun in April 1979 to be conscious of significant dates in my own spiritual odyssey, carefully recording them in my journal. Often the feast day celebrated on the Christian calendar shed amazing light on current events.

So now I looked with intense interest at the eruptions of the volcano in Washington, my home state.

When I heard that Mount Saint Helens had erupted for the second time, it was the date on the Christian calendar that struck me first, because it was such an important feast day. In fact, it was the birthday of institutional Christianity, the feast that celebrates the tongues of fire descending on the apostles to empower them to preach the Gospel.

Could it be merely accidental that the mountain had chosen the pope's birthday for its first massive eruption and then erupted again on this high feast of Pentecost, two significant Sundays in a row?

I felt the profound significance of the correspondence of dates. It could not be mere coincidence! But what did it *mean?* In the Gospels, Jesus admonishes us to watch and interpret the signs of the times. We had already heard the planet crying, environmentalists having alerted us to the results of pollution, the scars and mutilation of the land, the pollution of the waters, and the depletion and squandering of resources. But the mountain was different. Was Mount Saint Helens "speaking" in a special hidden language that could be deciphered by watching the Church calendar as I felt I had been instructed to do?

Bizarre as this may seem, the thought continued to haunt me. If it had been any other mountain, one I had never visited, or if Mount Saint Helens had borne a different name, or even if it had chosen a different date for its eruption, I might have been able to dismiss the nagging intuition to examine it more closely. But the correspondences and associations seemed too significant to be ignored. I was learning to honor any intuition that "spoke" to me, even when it seemed at first to defy rational explanation. Perhaps I was "stretching," looking too hard for meaning behind the events. But I honored the urgent need I felt to examine the events more closely.

First of all, the mountain bore the name of the mother of Constantine, the Roman emperor who in A.D. 315 officially legitimized the rapidly spreading church of the Christians. Saint Helena, who prayed fervently for her son's conversion to Christ, could easily be associated as the mother of the *institutional Church of Rome*, the powerful patriarchal institution organized in the image of the Roman Empire, with each regional diocese placed under the jurisdiction of an appointed imperial prelate.

The Church formed in the fourth century under Constantine; its power was later consolidated and strengthened by the emperor Theodosius, who changed the character of Christianity from a faith practiced in small, often persecuted, communities of "chapel homes" to an organized state religion, a hierarchical monolith with all the power at the top. This imperial Church underwrote and institutionalized the message of the Jewish charismatic Jesus, thereby ensuring that Christianity became the faith of the entire Roman Empire and ultimately of Western civilization.

In response to my inner prompting, I decided to watch Mount Saint Helens carefully and to record its further eruptions. Several weeks later, in early July 1980, I received another letter from Mary Beben, whose husband had recently been transferred from Puerto Rico to Tel Aviv. She stated that the 9th of Av on the Jewish calendar was an especially important day for our Emmanuel prayer community. On this day in Jerusalem faithful Jews go to the remaining Western Wall of their temple and lament its destruction—not once, but twice!—on this same date. The first temple, built by King Solomon in the tenth century B.C., was destroyed by Nebuchadnezzar in 586 B.C. and the second, built by King Herod the Great, was demolished by the commander of the victorious Roman legions on the same calendar date in A.D. 70.

In her letter sent to each member of the Emmanuel community, Mary requested that we keep a nine-day vigil for further enlightenment, culminating our community prayer on the 9th of Av, which on our calendar was July 22, 1980. On that date, she herself would represent our entire community at the Western Wall in Jerusalem, lamenting the lost temple with the Jewish people.

I did as she asked, deciding to end my vigil by attending mass on

July 22. The mass booklet in the pew contained the day's official readings: It was the feast day of Mary Magdalene.

The correspondence of dates did not speak strongly to me until the following morning. When I brought the newspaper in from the front steps, I found myself transfixed by the big full-color picture on the front page of the Nashville newspaper. Dense white smoke was billowing out of the "fire mountain." Mount Saint Helens had spoken again on July 22, 1980. She looked like Mount Sinai with her summit enshrouded in clouds. The smoking mountain *had* to be a theophany!

This mountain was attracting my attention to a very important message through a synchronicity of dates. For me, the "fire mountain" already represented the institutional Church, the Δ, now exploding from pressure within, causing devastation in the surrounding area. The beautiful and serene Spirit Lake had been tipped out in a metaphorical baptism of waters poured out into the land, not able to be confined any longer in the fonts of the Church, but poured out by the Great Dark Mother, Earth herself, having burst the "patriarchal" bonds. Now the "waters of truth" were being poured into other channels and back into the ground itself.

The Jewish date, the 9th of Av, was a significant clue in this interpretation—"9" representing "final judgment" in the ancient canon of sacred number.[1] The volcano Mount Saint Helens—now established in my mind as a symbol of the monolithic Roman institution that had proclaimed itself the New Jerusalem and the New Israel—was violently erupting, pouring devastation out for miles around. I was witnessing a prophetic proclamation of the destruction of the institutional Church, the bastion of Western civilization. The fire was coming from *within* the mountain, pouring out with catastrophic force. It was holocaust—the "burnt mountain" of Jeremiah's prophecy, and it seemed to be showing me the condition of the monolithic Church, self-destructing before my eyes.

The three years that followed this revelation were busy ones for me. My husband's job as a battalion commander in the elite 101st

"Screaming Eagles" Division at Fort Campbell required me to partic-
ipate in an endless stream of social events, command performances,
and activities related to his troops, in addition to caring for our five
children who ranged in age from five months to eleven years old
when we first arrived.

The whole three-year assignment has melted into mush in my
memory, except for a few highlights like the Amtrak train ride we
took out to visit my parents in Seattle one summer and a visit to
Ted's parents in Virginia, where I also got a chance to visit with several of my friends in Emmanuel. My whole life was one of trying to
juggle commitments and meet deadlines without being late to anything (a cardinal sin in the army!). I felt like a trained lioness, jump-
ing through fiery hoops, and experienced true compassion for the
caged beasts in the circus when it came to town. I was not *in* the
desert during this time; I *was* the desert.

During these months significant information related to the correspondence of the dates I had noted manifested, and I continued to
record it with interest. I learned that the Jewish calendar is based on
lunar months and so differs from ours. The chances of the 9th of Av
coinciding with the Feast of Saint Mary Magdalene on July 22 in any
given year are remote, since the coincidence of these dates varies
from year to year. But on that particular day in 1980, an extremely
significant ceremony was taking place simultaneously in southern
France. In the Cathedral of Mary Magdalene in the French town of
Saint-Maximin on the Mediterranean coast, six bishops of the
Roman Catholic Church and a special papal representative concele-
brated a unique liturgy and mass marking the seven hundredth
anniversary of the discovery of Mary Magdalene's grave in southern
France.

The liturgical celebration drew tens of thousands of pilgrims
from all over the world to the special "jubilee"—a "week" of seven
hundred years honoring the "other Mary" of the Gospel story. At the
exact same time—on July 22, 1980—faithful Jews in Jerusalem gathered to lament their ruined temple that has never been restored.
Mary Beben happened on that day to be standing and praying with

them at the Western Wall and had linked their lament for the temple to our own deep mourning for its loss.

And on that same day, while the Catholic Church was celebrating the feast day of Saint Mary Magdalene, Mount Saint Helens was erupting once more, the towering cloud of smoke signaling to those who had "eyes to see" that these events were somehow intimately interconnected. The entire earth seemed to be involved in a cosmic moment, in the same way that separate instruments in an orchestra touch at the same time the powerful peak of a crescendo.

This seemed to me a sign that somehow Mary Magdalene was a significant factor in the lost blueprint of the destroyed temple in Jerusalem and also, by association, in the destruction of the present Church establishment. In 1980, I did not yet understand her role, but I felt it must be of great importance because of the connected events I had witnessed.

Now, years later, the meaning behind these events is clear. The Temple in Jerusalem has not been rebuilt because the human family has lost *the sacred blueprint* of the floor plan, an archetypal blueprint already found at the core of each human being. It is also the blueprint for the "reign of God" or "kingdom of heaven" that Jesus proclaimed was already here in our midst: the sacred union of the opposites encoded by gematria in the Christian Gospels.[2] For the sacred number coded by gematria in the phrase "the grain of mustard seed" is 1746—identical to the sacred number used by Plato and philosophers to express the union of the opposite energies in the ancient canon. The mandala for this union is the ✡, the union of "the same and the other."[3]

This was the blueprint Mary had written about in her journal in 1973 when she was shown Jan's broken statue of Christ with the piece missing from its foundation. She was told then that a new blueprint was trying to emerge in human consciousness, but that the current model had first to be destroyed. As I now discovered, the blueprint that was manifesting was not "new." It was ancient, but tragically lost and then denied for the two millennia of Christianity.

In discussing this lost blueprint of the Temple, I do not intend to suggest that the geometric measurements of the Temple in Jerusalem are literally lost. Surely someone has by now reconstructed the actual physical measurements of Solomon's Temple. Instead, it is a case of the sacred geometry and the *symbolic meaning* of the measurements having been lost, the master plan of the design that is lamented still in the rituals of Freemasonry as the "lost word of the Master Mason." It is the blueprint for wholeness also manifested in the psyche of the human family that inhabits the planet. The Temple in Jerusalem was designed to contain the presence of Yahweh dwelling with his people in intimate union, an outward model of a mystical or inward reality: "God with (or within?) us."

The architects of the ancient cosmic temples deliberately balanced the influences of the masculine and feminine principles in their sacred geometry, reflecting the order in the cosmos in an attempt to bring harmony, blessing, and order to the society. Somehow, this understanding of wholeness and holiness flowing from the center of the temple has been distorted. Jesus, who understood and preached the correct blueprint, was called *tekton* in the original Greek of the New Testament, a word with connotations of "builder" or "engineer." The Greek word associated with him has been translated "carpenter" over the centuries, but its original meaning was that of "architect/designer" of the New Covenant, a role echoing the poignant Bridegroom prophecy of Isaiah: "As a young man marries a maiden, your *builder* shall marry you" (Isa. 62:5, emphasis mine).

The community is represented in this passage as the "Bride"— the sacred feminine. The covenant relationship between God and his people is to be modeled on the ancient understanding of the *hieros gamos*. This metaphor was later applied by Saint Paul to the relationship between Christ and his Bride, the Church.

After the destruction of the Temple of Solomon by the Babylonians in 586 B.C., the remnant of Israel was taken to Babylon where they remained captive for nearly seventy years. On their return, they were given permission to rebuild the destroyed temple in Jerusalem, the symbol of their covenant with Yahweh. "Does anyone remember the former glory of this house?"(Hag. 2:3). The prophet Haggai laments the destroyed temple. His question lingers: Does anyone today remember the ancient temple and its symbolism? Does anyone today think of the temple's Holy of Holies as the bridal chamber, symbolic of the human psyche, where the eternal Bridegroom is united with his Bride? In traditional Christian theological symbolism, the Church is the Bride, as Christ is the Bridegroom. We build churches, but we have watered down the life-giving power of the symbols and failed to communicate them to our children.

Because of the correspondence of the two significant dates, the 9th of Av and July 22, the volcano that erupted on the feast day of Mary Magdalene in 1980 is dramatically and irrevocably linked with the ruined temple in Jerusalem. I believe that the official repudiation of the "flesh and blood" feminine principle embodied in Mary Magdalene—the lost Bride—is a fracture in the very foundations of Christian teaching and that this fracture, if not corrected, will be the ultimate cause of its disintegration. This seems a foregone conclusion built into the word itself, since "integration"—male and female joined and honored as equal partners—is precisely the relationship that the theologians of the Church in Rome have until now refused, ever insisting on honoring an exclusively male image of God.

Seeing the theophany of the cloud hovering over Mount Saint Helens on July 22, 1980, and knowing that the mountain had spoken, I found my attention drawn specifically to Mary Magdalene because of the culmination of the Emmanuel community's prayer vigil on her feast day, a cosmic moment choreographed by the Lord of the Dance. The Native Americans of the Pacific Northwest call Mount Saint Helens the "Little Sister" which is also—uncannily—one of the treasured epithets of the Bride in the Song of Solomon. It seems that now and then we catch a glimpse of the Spirit that both orchestrates and indwells creation—the great "I AM." It is the voice of this Divine Being whose thundering command to Pharaoh has rippled down through the millennia, again and again breaking chains that bind us: "LET MY PEOPLE GO!"

During the months that followed the long, hot summer of 1980,

I was gradually becoming aware of my own bondage to the "sun god" and the burnout and utter exhaustion it was causing, the desert I was becoming. Until that point in my life I had willingly and even enthusiastically embraced the path of service to others, but now I was in pain, my health deteriorating, with no time for anything except meeting the bare requirements of my composite roles. I hardly had time to read nursery rhymes to my littlest sons and felt totally fragmented by the demands on my time and energy. In my unconscious state, I felt impelled to begin sewing a quilt. It was not until months later, when it was nearly done, that I realized that I had been trying to unite shredded pieces of my life into some sort of coherent whole. I began to see how the outer events of my life shed light on the inner ones and to understand the concept of "waking up" to reality.

The eruption of Mount Saint Helens on Mary Magdalene's feast day in 1980 urged me to learn all I could about the Mary who was so intimately connected with Jesus. I studied, read, and prayed over the Magdalene, eventually uncovering numerous surprising details. This intimate friend of Jesus had gradually been written out of the Christian story, devalued by centuries of tradition naming her prostitute, in spite of her special prominence in all four of the canonical Gospels. No one seemed to care that Mary of Bethany, who sat at Jesus' feet and drank in his teachings (Luke 10:39) and who anointed Jesus at the banquet at Bethany (John 12), was the "woman with the alabaster jar," even though Jesus himself stated that the story of his anointing for burial would be "told and retold in memory of her" (Mark 14:9; Matt. 26:13).

In a sixth-century sermon delivered at the basilica of Saint Clement in Rome, Pope Saint Gregory stated his belief that Mary of Bethany and Mary Magdalene were one and the same person, to be identified with the woman who anointed Jesus in all four Gospels,[4] probably articulating the prevailing view of Christians in Western Europe. On the feast of "the Magdalene," the official readings of the Roman Catholic liturgy are taken from the Song of Songs, virtually equating her with the dark Bride. "Set me as a seal on your heart, a seal on your arm," the Bride enjoins her lover (Cant. 8:6). This verse was already very familiar to me, for the members of Emmanuel had included it in our communal prayer of consecration, written at our retreat in 1979.

The twelfth-century bishop and mystic Saint Bernard of Clairvaux equates Mary of Bethany with that Bride as well, following the ancient Church tradition of the second-century exegetes Hippolytus of Rome and Origen. In pamphlets found in churches in southern France, Martha and the "Madeleine" (Magdalene) are explicitly referred to as the "sisters of Lazarus." Uncannily, as I later realized, the second eruption of the volcano on May 25, 1980 (Pentecost Sunday!) had also coincided with the culmination of the yearly Gypsy festival honoring the black Saint Sarah and her traveling companions—the three Marys—in the little French coastal town of Les Saintes-Maries-de-la-Mer.

Over the years I have often encountered the admonition of the prophet Isaiah, "When you see the signal raised upon the mountain, LOOK! and when you hear the trumpet, LISTEN!" (Isa. 18:3). The eruptions of Mount Saint Helen's in 1980 were for me a "signal raised upon the mountain," immensely important for my developing consciousness of the fatal flaw in Christianity because they so radically linked the holocaust of the Catholic Church and the ruined walls of the Temple in Jerusalem with Mary Magdalene, pointing specifically to her as the missing piece of the lost blueprint—the ✡.

I came to understand that a revised interpretation of Christian truths was needed, along with a deeper look at the doctrine concerning the full humanity of Jesus. The significant role of Mary Magdalene, who—I am convinced beyond any doubt—embodies the eternal feminine as Bride, has been misunderstood and neglected, perhaps even deliberately obscured, and needs to be reexamined. In releasing her from her bondage and restoring her to the partnership mandala, we will restore the archetypal balance of feminine and masculine— "on earth as it is in heaven"—at the same time restoring the feminine to a place of honor in our own lives.

In thinking about the impact of the tragic loss of Magdalene, I began to realize that I had always honored my role as mother to my children but had not fully grasped my role as partner to my husband, having had no model for this all-important relationship in my religious indoctrination. What a different relationship we might have developed together, I sensed, if we had not both been so totally oriented toward meeting the demands of his career and those of our children.

Proclaiming the Mary, the mother of Jesus, as "Co-Redemptrix" could place the feminine in an honored role with Christ, I realized. But let it not preempt the reclaiming of Mary the Magdalene, the forgotten Bride, who was in the beginning and remains the Beloved of Christ, the archetypal Bridegroom. Their true partnership is the celestial model with healing in its wings!

The mountain has spoken. After years of pondering its message, I now bear witness to its prophetic voice. When you visit Mount Saint Helens, take off your shoes: The place where you are standing is holy ground.

CHAPTER VI

OUR LADY OF THE QUEST

Come to me, all you that yearn for me and be filled with my fruits. You will remember me as sweeter than honey . . .(Sirach 24:18)

In June 1983 we moved back to Alexandria, Virginia, and in September, Ann Requa, a friend from my college years, visited me there. During our visit, she recommended a book she had found recently in the library where she worked, thinking that with my background in medieval European studies and my interest in the Bible and in the origins of Christianity, I might be intrigued by it.

I went to the local library and found the book Ann had recommended. When I took it off the shelf and read the synopsis on the back cover, I was shocked that she had ever thought I might be even remotely interested! At the time, I was orthodox to the core, both in belief and in practice of my Roman Catholic faith, the "faith of our fathers." I taught religious education classes for our local parish and still corresponded closely with my friends in the Emmanuel community, two of whom were now Roman Catholic priests. I fumbled with the book, trying so hard to put it back on the shelf that I almost dropped it. Like the proverbial "hot potato," it seemed to be burning my fingers. The thesis of the book was heresy: the suggestion that Jesus and Mary Magdalene were married and had a child. The title of the book was *Holy Blood, Holy Grail.*[1]

I escaped from the library as fast as I could. I did not want to know anything that was at variance with teachings of the magisterium of the Roman Catholic Church. Over the next weeks and months, I tried desperately to forget what I had read on the back cover of the book, but it would not go away. I remembered the myths of Pandora's box and Bluebeard's wives—the ugly fate of the idly curious—but in the back of my mind was the haunting question: "Is there any chance that what the authors proclaimed might be true?"

I tried to ignore the question and to concentrate on my daily routines of diapers, dishes, and soccer car pools. I was afraid to tell my friends in Emmanuel about my encounter with the heresy of the "sangraal"—the Holy Grail. I tried to live my life as if nothing had changed, but it was futile. Everything had changed. What if the religious doctrines I had adhered to all my life were wrong? I wondered. What if someone had lied? Whom could I trust? What did they know—the patriarchs who had formed the doctrines of Christianity? And when did they know it? Was there any way to really know the truth? And why had we never heard even the faintest rumor of this marriage? My life looked the same on the outside, but my inner life was in seething turmoil.

Another friend, about eighteen months later, suggested that I read a book written by David Yallop called In God's Name.[2] This time when I found the book in the library, I checked it out. I was more appalled at each succeeding page, but I could not put the book down. At the request of the private secretary and housekeeper of the dead pontiff, the author had investigated the alleged 1978 murder of Pope John Paul I, presumably by individuals involved in the ugly scandals surrounding the official Vatican bank.

As I have mentioned, the possible murder of the first Pope John Paul had already been brought to the attention of our Emmanuel prayer community, whose members had recorded prophetic verses concerning the assassination of the "high priest" and the plundering of the "temple treasury" as early as 1974. The book In God's Name suggested that the Romans and the priests had collaborated to execute this "thirty-three-day" pope (just as these same factions had conspired to execute the "thirty-three-year-old" Jesus two millennia before!). The prophecies the community Emmanuel had received from 1974 to 1978 about the corruption of the temple, the robbing of the treasury, and the cutting down of the Anointed One seemed to have crystallized in one catastrophic event—the murder of the anointed "high priest," Luciano Albino—Pope John Paul I.

It was April 1985 when I read *In God's Name*. I was extremely disillusioned by the alleged Vatican scandals and their cover-up by the corrupt ecclesiastical hierarchy. I began to wonder what other elephants and camels I would find hidden under their expensive Vatican rugs! Finally, I decided that the book my friend Ann had recommended eighteen months before could not distress me any more deeply than the book I had just read. So on my next visit to the library, I returned Yallop's book and checked out *Holy Blood, Holy Grail*.

I was wrong. The second book was infinitely more distressing than the first; it was devastating. The mere thought that the Church hierarchy could have hidden—even suppressed—so much significant evidence for the fact that Jesus was married made me feel physically ill. For months thereafter it tormented me. The deliberate withholding of this information would constitute severe abuse of the entire body of Christian believers—an abuse of their trust and ultimately also of their well-being!

Where was truth? I wondered. Could we believe any of the doctrines we had been taught? How could we know if they were true? The book was so disturbing that I was reluctant to tell anyone about its allegations, not even my best friends in the Emmanuel community. I was concerned that it would frighten them and erode their faith in the doctrines and traditions of Christianity. I remembered the Gospel passage about the millstone around the neck of the one who destroys the faith of the little ones, and I was afraid. I struggled with the burden alone for as long as I could bear it.

In the closing weeks of 1985 my friend and "kinswoman" Mary Beben moved from New York to Virginia with her husband and their youngest son. I had not yet told her about the book *In God's Name*, but finally I found the courage to mention its scandalous premise to her. Mary had not read the book, but she was concerned because it had upset me so much. We decided to pray together about David Yallop's book and its implications, and we finally found an opportunity to meet on the morning of January 28, 1986.

The day had been declared a "snow day" in Fairfax County, so all five of my children were home from school, playing in our basement rec room and watching television. Undeterred by the meager three-inch snowfall, Mary drove over as planned to spend the day with me, bringing her small son to play with my children. They were just pulling into the driveway, and I had gone out to greet them, when Kate exploded out of the house behind me.

"MOMMY! The space shuttle just blew up!!"

Mary and I stared at one another in shocked disbelief. We ran with our children downstairs and watched in horror the televised replay of the fireball that snatched away the *Challenger* spacecraft and its seven passengers. Over and over the film's replay showed us the terrifying sequence of the accident.

Returning to our senses, Mary and I climbed the stairs to the kitchen and spent the rest of that snow-bound January day in sober prayer for enlightenment about the meaning of the event we had witnessed. I also showed Mary a book I had just borrowed from the library about Jewish mysticism, which explained the mystical Tree of Life of the Cabala and discussed the twin pillars of the Temple—left and right—and their relationship to the tree.

Together we pored over this material that we had not ever studied before. Only days later did it dawn on us that the symbolism of the twin pillars had direct bearing on the *Challenger* accident—that we were actually holding in our hands the key to understanding the tragic event.

It took us several weeks to gather up the shattered pieces of the accident into a composite, coherent picture.

At home later that same evening, my friend began reading my copy of *In God's Name*. After reading only the first chapter, she was thoroughly shaken, finally understanding for the first time why the

Emmanuel community had been shown the text from Daniel 9:26 at our reunion in August 1977—exactly one year prior to the election of Pope John Paul I.

Feeling shattered by the evidence recounted, Mary continued to read Yallop's book, remembering the verses received by the members of the Emmanuel community over a period of twelve years about the corruption and plunder of the Temple and the murder of the anointed high priest. She no longer doubted that the events surrounding the death of John Paul I were suspicious. At the very least there had been a massive and inexcusable cover-up of the facts, including the ugly scandal surrounding the Vatican bank—a massive cover-up that had occurred with the full collusion of the Church hierarchy. When Mary told me of her feelings, I was comforted to know that she now saw what I had already seen—the fulfillment of the early prophecies of the Emmanuel community. At least I was no longer alone in my misery.

For both Mary and me, a process of mourning set in during those days in the winter of 1986. It was the beginning of a great disillusionment and an enormous loss of our whole system of reality and identity. We could no longer mouth the party line, no longer refrain from questioning, no longer feel comfortable teaching Roman Catholic doctrine to children in religious education classes. The solid rock of Peter's Church on which we had based our lives was crumbling.

We began to feel sad and dry when we attended mass or participated in other religious rituals. Something felt wrong. We had believed that the fathers of the Church had passed on to us the truth—the whole truth and nothing but the truth. We had trusted them with our lives and with our eternal salvation, believing everything they had taught us. And now that trust was shattered. But at the same time we felt the Spirit was helping us to awaken from an unreal, whitewashed image of the Church in which we had believed from our youth, and so we renewed our trust in the Holy Spirit and continued to share our journey with one another.

In the days that followed, Mary and I examined the whole tragic saga of the *Challenger* launch in detail because it had been brought so radically to our attention. Just as a rocketship is a vessel of the modern age, carrying its passengers into realms unknown, a ship—"Peter's bark"—has often been used as a symbol for the Church of Peter, navigating through two millennia of storms and winds.

The fatal launch of *Challenger* had taken place on the feast of Saint Thomas Aquinas, one of the great articulators of Christian doctrine, in our minds throwing a spotlight on *Challenger* as a symbol for the Roman Catholic Church. But we were shocked, under the circumstances, to discover that Saint Thomas Aquinas is the patron saint of sudden death. In researching the events surrounding the *Challenger* incident, I discovered that he actually died while giving a talk to monks at a monastery where he was an overnight guest. He was interpreting for them a passage about the Bride from the Song of Songs when he suffered his fatal stroke. This thirteenth-century "father," whose published teachings helped to strengthen the patriarchal power of the Church, had retracted those same erudite works shortly before his death, pronouncing them "mere straw," and died while discoursing on the Hebrew love poem celebrating the Sacred Marriage![3]

The National Aeronautics and Space Administration (NASA)'s investigators of the *Challenger* tragedy soon agreed that the fatal fault lay in the right booster rocket, specifically in the "O-rings" that were supposed to be a protective sheath for the fuel rods used to propel the spacecraft. The unexpectedly extreme cold of the previous night had cracked the O-rings. The *right* booster rocket seemed the perfect symbol of the high-tech, left-brain, masculine-oriented thinking of Western society. And its symbolism was even more appropriate when applied to the Roman Catholic Church, bereft of the feminine covering that should have been in place for its own protection, symbolized by the cracked O-rings designed to sheathe the fuel rods of the booster rocket. The Jewish Cabala's Tree of Life and the twin pillars of the Jewish temple we were discussing on the day of the disaster provided clues we needed to interpret these symbols.

The top scientific administrators at NASA who had allowed the launch of *Challenger* did not take into sufficient account the severe stress to the O-rings imposed by the overnight freezing temperatures. According to recently published accounts, officials had feared a problem arising from the cold but had not wanted to postpone the launch yet again, causing embarrassing loss of face for their space program. They had weighed the warnings and decided to take the risk.

And therein lies the prophetic understanding my friend and I were given of the disaster in store for the Church: the cold, rigid, and intolerant mindset of the hierarchy has frozen out the feminine for millennia, leaving the institution vulnerable to disaster.

More prophetic parallels with the Church were revealed as we examined further details of the *Challenger* launch. Seven people perished aboard the spacecraft, six crew members and a teacher named Christa McAulliffe. The woman named for Christ had come from Saint Peter's parish; the other woman on board the flawed space shuttle was a daughter of Judaism—a scientist named Judith. We knew the symbolic properties of the number seven—the number for the Holy Spirit, the mystical number signifying eternity and completeness: There are seven gifts of the Holy Spirit, seven days in a week, and seven times seventy occasions for forgiveness. The multi-ethnic diversity of the personnel aboard *Challenger* was further confirmation that the crew of the lost spacecraft represented the entire human family of God.

The tragedy of the space shuttle was personally devastating. It was like hearing a trumpet blast that no one else could hear, a trumpet that blared, "LOOK at these events! SEE and REMEMBER! Weigh them in your heart. Do not let them pass by lightly, but contemplate and record all that you witness! Above all, let this sacrifice not be wasted!"

Mary and I sensed that we were seeing a powerful sign for the Church itself. The demise of the institution as we know it might come just as suddenly and painfully for those who feel sheltered in it. There would come a moment when the stresses would become too great and the institutional walls would not stand up to the test because of the flaw in its structure—the gigantic fatal flaw that is the *missing feminine.*

This feminine balance has been trained out of the men as well as the women of the Church, and all are suffering the fatal wound. We knew that we saw the impending "shipwreck" of the Church, a shipwreck already happening one life at a time and perhaps a massive catastrophe for the faith itself, but we felt helpless to avert it. Who would listen to mere housewives?

Certainly not the vested authorities in Rome! We were not "experts" nor did we have doctorates in theology. I characterize myself as a "kitchen-sink contemplative"; many of my deepest inspirations have occurred while doing the dishes or peeling potatoes. I feel a particular affinity for Brother Lawrence, the mystic lay brother who was a scullion in a European monastery. The spiritual classic *The Practice of the Presence of God,* based on his teachings, was always my favorite book on the Christian way, rooted in humble service to others.

On the night of January 28, I had opened my Bible looking for comfort and guidance and had encountered verses from Isaiah 21: "The watchers on the watchtower" proclaim the news: "Fallen, fallen is Babylon, and all the images of her gods are smashed to the ground." The biblical Babylon was the sinful, idolatrous, sun-worshiping capital of the ancient Near East. At the time I did not yet understand the archetypal meaning of Babylon—the city of sun-worship—or fully realize what her idols were, but I faithfully recorded the date and the passage in my journal and went heavy-hearted to bed.

A few weeks later, I mustered enough courage to share with Mary the heretical thesis of *Holy Blood, Holy Grail,* something that I had deliberately avoided doing because I had not wanted to shake her foundations any further. She was reluctant to listen, let alone believe that an alternative version of the life of Jesus was possible. But we had been through so much together by now that she understood that the issue was of grave importance to me. It just seemed so utterly fantastic and farfetched to both of us that Jesus might have been married! How could we not have heard of it before? How could the Church itself not know? Surely *someone* in authority would have told us before now! Mary thought the whole idea preposterous.

Meanwhile, I was comforted by her strong reaction. Perhaps she was right—surely they would have told us information as important as this! But still the idea would not go away. Somehow I needed to get to the bottom of it.

Several days later, I sat down on my living room sofa with my Bible, my journal, and a copy of *Holy Blood, Holy Grail.* I began to pray. I told Jesus that I would burn the book on my friend's recommendation, but first I wanted to know whatever he himself wanted to show me about it.

The biblical passages I received in prayer that afternoon were as riveting as they were unexpected. I let my Bible fall open to a random page and stared down at the frontispiece of the New Testament. It stated "New Testament . . . A REVISION . . ."

The Emmanuel prayer community had been told nearly ten years before that we would have a part in rewriting Holy Scripture. Orthodox and conservative as we were, we had assumed that Emmanuel's members would have a modern-day counterpart of the experience of the Living God celebrated by the early Christians and that someday we would be called to bear witness to it. But now I was being shown an entirely new understanding of that prophecy. I remember thinking as I looked down at the page in my Bible, *Lord, do you mean that we need a revision of* this *New Testament?* I was frightened at the mere idea; it seemed blatantly, outrageously presumptuous!

I closed my Bible and prayed for clarification: "In what way does the New Testament need to be revised?" I asked. Then I opened my Bible again, this time to find that the page before me was from the Second Book of Kings. I noticed with relief that it was not a New Testament passage. How could it be even vaguely relevant? Then I read a line from the upper right-hand column, to which my thumb seemed to be pointing: "Restore my wife whom I espoused to me . . ."

The impact of the line began to dawn on me. Of course, the

passage in Kings was totally out of context. King David was demanding the return his wife, Michol, who was Saul's daughter. But in light of the question I had asked, the line seemed to be Christ's answer to me in that moment. I was shaken. Confirmation of his marriage was the last thing I had expected. Yet there could not possibly be any other page in my entire 1500-page Bible on which this poignantly significant injunction was printed!

But, still, I was cautious, not wanting to accept the evidence before my eyes. Again I prayed for enlightenment, orthodox to the last: "Lord, I know you have a Bride, the Church. Is that the wife you mean me to restore?" Once again, with growing temerity, I opened my Bible. Marked by my thumb on the page before me was Galatians 4:22-24:

> For it is written that Abraham had two sons, one by
> the slave-girl and the other by a free woman. And the son
> of the slave-girl was born according to the flesh, but the
> son of the free woman in virtue of the promise. This is said
> by way of allegory.

The truth-prickles crawled down my spine. I felt convinced that the "allegory" mentioned in the passage from Galatians referred to Jesus and that the Scripture passage I had been given was affirming that he had two offspring: one, the Church, "in virtue of the promise," and the other "of the flesh."

One of the adages by which I have lived is that God is a surprise. When God seems to be saying something that you never expected to hear, chances are it is important. At least, you should not just ignore it, hoping it will go away. I decided to honor what I had been shown in the pages of my Bible, no matter how preposterous it sounded, at least until such time as I could prove it wrong.

My hands were shaking a few mintues later when I dialed Mary's phone number. I poured out to her the story of the questions I had asked and the passages in my Bible I had randomly encountered, along with the message I had understood. I could tell she was unhappy with what I was saying. She suggested that perhaps the information needed to be applied to my inner work rather than to the whole Church— that maybe it was my inner bride that needed to be restored. She warned me that if I did not find a way to deal with this issue, it would find a way to break through. She knew much more about Carl Jung's work and about spirituality and psychology than I did, so I tried to accept her interpretation. She was in adamant denial that the message I had received was for the entire Church, but she agreed to pray about it. I hung up the telephone.

Two days later Mary called me back. She had been having plumbing problems ever since their family's move to Virginia in early December. For no discernible reason, the toilet in the master bathroom had been slowly leaking around its base. Her husband had replaced the caulking and they had tried everything they could think of, but the leak continued.

They finally called a plumber, who was equally baffled and spent some time thoroughly examining the toilet fixture until he discovered a hairline crack in the very base of the bowl. He removed the fractured bowl and installed a new one of the same make and style. They had all felt sure the problem was solved.

However, the next morning Mary discovered that the slow leak was still there. She couldn't believe it! She got down on her knees to examine the base of the toilet bowl and found—sure enough— another hairline fracture similar to the one around the base of the first toilet bowl! At the same time she happened to notice the name of the manufacturer, a single word printed inside the leaking porcelain bowl: "Church."

I didn't know whether to laugh—or cry! Now we both clearly and irrevocably understood that the crack in the foundation of the Christian Church was the lost feminine, the Bride.

The shattered statue of Jesus that Jan and her husband had glued together back at West Point in 1973 had had a piece missing from the foundation. The right booster rocket of the spaceship *Challenger* also had had a critical and fatal flaw. We realized that there was a common message in these seemingly unconnected events. There was something missing, something that from the beginning had kept the Church from reflecting and radiating peace and holiness throughout the world, something that was now threatening to blow up the entire institution, something that kept it from holding water.

That missing piece has repeatedly been shown to me and to others to be the lost feminine principle in Christianity, an institution that has honored the spirit and intellect of humankind while scorning and repudiating the flesh, the sacred container of the Spirit. The vessel, scorned, has become a cracked cistern. The Church has been built over a tragic flaw in its very foundation: the Bride denied. No wonder statues of the Madonna shed tears in shrines worldwide! Even the stones cry out!

In addressing this issue, I gradually began to realize that women, including myself, have been denied our true heritage. Our ways of being, of knowing, of relating have been scorned for millennia, our advice repudiated, our gifts spurned, our dreams thwarted.

This neglected feminine principle of "Wisdom/Sophia" is perhaps best represented by the image of the Black Madonna of Czestochowa to whom the Emmanuel community had been officially consecrated on May 29, 1979. At the time we did not understand her inscrutable dark image, but we knew she was calling us, and we had prayed for her support and patronage. I was particularly haunted by her eyes.

At our consecration retreat in 1979, Faye, one of the original members of the Emmanuel community, had brought us a verse from the Song of Songs: "Set me as a seal on your heart, a seal on your arm." At her calm insistence, we had written this verse into our community's prayer of consecration, but at the time we did not realize that this verse from the Canticle was once part of the official liturgy—not for a Marian feast day of the Blessed Virgin, however, *but for the feast of Saint Mary Magdalene!* There was so much we did not know in 1979, when we committed ourselves to the specific purpose of praying for the purification and healing of the Roman Catholic Church and its priests. But now it was February 1986, *seven years* later, and we had witnessed the sign on the mountain and the explosion of *Challenger*.

From that day when Mary and I fully realized that the foundation of the Church was fatally flawed, I felt impelled to research the thesis of *Holy Blood, Holy Grail* from every possible angle. Something about it kept calling to me, "ringing a bell" that seemed an echo of details I already knew but couldn't quite remember.

And so, following my intuition, I embarked on the solemn quest for the truth concerning the Holy Grail. I borrowed books from the library, making special requests through interlibrary loan and searching bibliographies for additional suggested reading. I was grateful for my academic background in literature and research tools it had provided. Often I studied until the early morning hours. I was still keeping house for my husband and five children, meeting the requirements of a military wife and mother, but now I had another mission as well, one that aroused in me a deep burning passion. I wanted to know the truth concerning the marriage of Jesus and Mary Magdalene.

Being basically reason oriented, I set out to test what my faith and intuition had revealed. Direct revelation had confirmed the "heretical" thesis that I had wanted to deny, but I was not ready to believe it without first examining all the sources available; I could not just accept intuition and inspiration alone without confirming by researching available records. It was clear that the "Grail heresy"— that Jesus had been married and that Mary Magdalene had brought a child of his to Gaul—existed, and had existed in Europe for a long time. My question was, *Why? What was at the heart of this heresy, and why was it so prevalent in the Middle Ages?* My first desire had been to debunk the tenets of the Grail heresy. But I sensed that where there is so much smoke, there is often fire.

In researching the question, I soon discovered that evidence of the belief of Jesus' marriage was far more widespread than I would have imagined. I examined medieval art works and literature, the earliest Grail legends, rituals of Freemasonry, myths, and symbols. I combed libraries and requested numerous obscure volumes, reading anything that might be remotely relevant. Gradually it became clear that there was indeed a mountain of circumstantial evidence for the marriage of Jesus—too much evidence to allow the tenets of the medieval Grail heresy to be ignored.

In July 1986 our family moved from Alexandria, Virginia, to my husband's new assignment in Nashville, Tennessee. One day soon after the moving crew abandoned me to a house full of boxes, I was unpacking books and shelving them. In my hands was a book I had not seen for months, one I had ordered on an impulse years before because it had been mentioned by British esotericist John Michell in his work on Atlantis.

The book I was holding was Harold Bayley's *The Lost Language of Symbolism.*[4] I had been fascinated by it when I read it in 1976. And now I opened it and began to thumb idly through its pages. On virtually every leaf were drawings of medieval watermarks found in antique European Bibles published between 1280 and 1600.

The watermarks were emblems imbedded in the paper itself, religious symbols of medieval papermakers, and were only visible when the pages were held up to the light.[5] *What an ingenious device for hiding their faith!* I thought, knowing that the alternative Church of the Holy Grail relied for their salvation on illumination and personal encounter with the true light of Christ, rather than on the indoctrination and sacraments of the Roman Church. The symbolic images of the watermarks—unicorns, chalices, lions, towers and palms—literally sang to me of the Grail and of the heretics of southern France, so ruthlessly persecuted by the long arm of the Inquisition during the early thirteenth century.[6]

Rediscovering the watermarks at this time was a powerful synchronicity. Suddenly I realized why the secrets of the Grail heresy had spoken so powerfully to me for so many months. I had already encountered them years before in this obscure book of medieval emblems, the watermarks of the heretical papermakers containing fossils of their faith. No wonder the Grail symbols had felt like old friends calling to me from the depths of my unconscious. They were!

The more I investigated the legends surrounding the Holy Grail, the more convinced I became of its importance. Everywhere I was finding confirmation of the basic tenet of the heresy of the Holy Grail—that Mary Magdalene was the Beloved of Christ. I sometimes felt as if my hair had caught fire! Either Jesus really had been married or else a deliberate all-out attempt had been made by "heretics" in the Middle Ages to restore the lost feminine principle to the Christian paradigm because they sensed an urgent necessity to balance the underlying myth of their faith. *Which was it?*

The revealing symbolism in European art and literature was incredibly widespread. Numerous enigmas of European culture were suddenly illuminated by the tenets of the Grail heresy. And my own synchronicities uncannily and consistently confirmed it. I was caught up in a quest of immeasurable dimensions, running now, nearly breathless, following leads from an ever-growing number of sources, trying to piece Magdalene's story back together, trying to restore the mandala of the "Sacred Marriage" lost to Christianity for millennia. There was no turning back!

CHAPTER VII

THE FALL OF BABYLON

Fallen, fallen is Babylon and all the images of her gods are smashed to the ground.(Isa. 21:9b)

When we first realized we were seeing prophetic images of the holocaust to be suffered by the Church in the *Challenger* blast and in the fierce eruption of Mount Saint Helens, Mary and I did not think in terms of the personal holocaust that would be suffered in our own psyches. That was something we would learn about only though direct experience. What follows here is a painful personal witness to the devastation brought about by this "sudden death" of my own belief system. Looking back I see parallels in the practice of medieval alchemy, turning lead into gold, and I realize that it was part of a spiritual process, but at the time it was excruciating—the "dark night" of my soul.

Over an extended period, I had been in a crucible, in turmoil over the discoveries my research had revealed. I knew with ever-growing certainty that something precious had been missing since the very dawn of the Christian era. I continued to research the tenets and legacy of the medieval heretics, including art books that contained a wealth of fascinating information. I pored over them intently, looking for symbols of the forgotten heresy of the Grail. On December 6, 1986, while I was browsing through books displayed on the sale table in our local bookstore, I noticed a book that had obvious Grail symbolism on the cover: spears, chalices, and a budding staff. Excited and curious, I picked up the book. The title was *The Tarot*,[1] and the volume contained numerous illustrations of tarot cards from various centuries.

I gazed at the inside cover of the book I was holding. I had never before seen pictures of tarot cards, and in December 1986 was so naive about esoteric material I didn't even know what the tarot was! But when I looked at the pen-and-ink outline sketches of the Charles VI tarot trumps, one of the earliest known decks, printed across the opening pages of the book, I felt little prickles of recognition going down my spine. I did not know anything at all about the tarot trumps, but I knew a vast amount about the Church of the Holy Grail, and I knew without question that the tarot was a visual catechism of the Albigensian heresy of the Holy Grail.[2]

I remember now that I had read somewhere, probably in Harold Bayley's other significant work, entitled *New Light on the Renaissance*, that traveling troupes of minstrels and entertainers in the Middle Ages were accused of spreading the Albigensian heresy. Yet there before me was *proof* of this theory: the tarot trumps! Later I discovered that the word *trompe* in old French means "trumpet," and I realized that these *trompes* were for me like the trumpets of Joshua that brought down the walls of Jericho. The horn was a medieval symbol for heretical preaching, which, like the horn of the French epic-hero Roland, could split rock, and the rock that the symbolic horn of heresy split would naturally be Peter's rock, the Church of Rome. "When the trumpet blows, listen!" commands Isaiah 18:3b. I was hearing trumpets blast just looking at those pictures!

The very first card that caught my eye was The Hermit. I remember looking at this image for the first time, not knowing that it was called The Hermit, and thinking, *I wonder what Peter the Hermit is doing here!* I knew intuitively that the card represented Peter, the monk who had gone from town to town in the closing decade of the eleventh century stirring up enthusiasm for the Crusade to win Jerusalem back from the Saracens. The hermit in the picture was not carrying a lantern, as the relevant text in the book suggested; he was holding an *hourglass*. Peter's message to the townspeople of Christendom had been one of urgency: "Now it is time." A full millennium had passed since the Roman legions' destruction of Jerusalem. It was time to reclaim the Holy City.

The hour glass in the hermit's hand, however, did not provide the definitive hint as to his identity. I had been playing a "hidden pictures" game with my children for years and had become adept at finding articles hidden in pictures. The essential clue was the large rock formation along the right side of the trump card, for Peter's name, as every Christian child must learn, means "rock."

Another card from the major arcana of the Charles VI tarot deck that startled me that day pictured a knight carrying a battle-ax, presumably returning with the spoils of war, but the conveyance closely resembled a tabernacle—or a hearse draped in cloth. The knight was standing with one foot on a decorative emblem shaped like the capital letter *I*, and next to it was a curved device forming the letter *C*. Together the two letters *IC* form the Latin initials of "Iesu Christi."

I did not know then that this tarot trump is commonly called The Charioteer. Obviously it pictured a Templar, returning with the spoils of war from the Crusade to Jerusalem. The Knights of the Temple of Solomon was a military order founded in Jerusalem in the early years of the twelfth century during the occupation of the Holy City by Christian knights. Soldier-clerics of this order are rumored to have brought back important treasure excavated from the ruins of Solomon's Temple in Jerusalem, treasure that was reputed to include secrets relating to Jesus that could destroy the credibility of the Church of Rome.

It is whispered in Europe that the Knights of the Temple found the tomb of Jesus and brought an ossuary containing his bones back to France, hence their well-known symbol of the skull and crossed bones. Of course, although this seems to have been a belief of the medieval Knights Templar, it would be anathema to the Catholic Church because it denies the doctrine of the bodily ascension of Christ into heaven, a significant tenet of Roman Catholic belief.

I already suspected that the secret treasure of the Templars was the contents of the treasury and archives found under the ruined Temple in Jerusalem, including perhaps important documents relating to the first generation of the Christian community, authentic documents buried before the Temple was destroyed in A.D. 70. Looking at this trump card, I intuited that the secret treasure was not confined to precious artifacts of gold; it was much more significant and threatening than mere riches. It concerned doctrines of the full humanity of Jesus Christ and the earliest version of the Christian story.

Still another tarot card attracted my interest on the day of my first encounter: the twelfth trump, The Hanged Man. Of course, I did not yet know it was called that because I had not yet read the author's written explanation of the cards. I did not yet know the names of any of the tarot trumps or their inferred meanings. But I had been researching the Grail heresy in depth, and I recognized that these cards, the trumps from the Charles VI deck, formed its catechism. I saw the man suspended by his foot from a crossbar supported by two rugged staffs, and I knew without words that he represented the "tortured Templar."

Only a few weeks earlier I had seen a painting depicting the scene of torture of the Knights Templar. The text of the book in which the picture appeared hinted at heinous tortures, including sexual tortures, to which the Templars were subjected by the Inquisition in its attempt to wrest from them their treasure. And as I had already learned, the leg, thigh, or foot is the universal euphemism for the phallus in art and literature.

The theme of the "wounded king" most often represents him as lame or crippled, a cryptic symbolic reference to his impotence rather than to an actual injury to his leg. In all ancient myth, including the story of King David, sexual potency is a necessary attribute for kingship because it ensures the fertility and well-being of the kingdom. When the king is no longer able to regenerate, the people become sick and desolated; the land becomes wasted, and the flowers and trees no longer blossom. The domain of the wounded king in the Grail legends suffers this same plight because the Grail is lost.

On the tarot trump, the other leg of the hanged man is bent and his tunic draped to form a fleur-de-lis, the symbol for the Merovingian bloodline claimed to be descended from the child of Jesus and Mary Magdalene. The French King Louis XI (ruled 1463–1481) is said to have claimed descent from Mary Magdalene. Perhaps this lineage is at the root of the term "blue-blooded," since blue is "celestial" and denotes divinity.

The "tortured Templar" on the tarot trump is pictured holding money bags, one in each hand. He is custodian of the secret treasure of the Templars never divulged to the Inquisition. The secret of the Templars was of esoteric value—very likely linked with the genealogies of the Merovingians and the true doctrines of the early Christians rather than with material assets of the denounced order liquidated by decree in 1307.[3]

Other cards contained further symbols of the heresy. The cupids in the card called The Lovers, the sixth trump, have red X's across their chests, an esoteric symbol used to identify the "Church of Amor"—the alternative Christian church of medieval Europe. The alternative nature of this other church was inherent in its name, since "Amor" is "Roma" spelled backward. The archetypal symbols for male and female, the Λ and the V, joined together form the letter X. This was the same mark mentioned in the Latin translations of Ezekiel 9:4, used to mark the foreheads of the enlightened ones who mourn over Jerusalem: "Pass through the city and mark an X on the foreheads of those who moan and groan over all the abominations that are practiced within it." According to Harold Bayley's *The Lost Language of Symbolism*, the letter X was used by the medieval heretics to represent "lux," or "enlightenment." The Greek letters for the Latin word *lux*—Λ, V, and X—were all present in the symbol, summed up in the letter X.[4]

The Grail heresy, according to Michael Baigent and the two friends who coauthored *Holy Blood, Holy Grail*, included the belief that the bloodline of Jesus continued to flow in the veins of certain European families who safeguarded their genealogies through the centuries. They called themselves "the Vine," a reference to their

Davidic descent. In the Hebrew Bible, the prophet Isaiah refers to the House of Israel as God's "vineyard," and declares "the men of Judah are his cherished plant" (Isa. 5:7). These families seem to have been related by blood to the Merovingian kings as well.

And so, this trump card of the Charles VI tarot deck could appropriately be called The Vine. The couples are shown in procession, suggestive of their lineage. The woman in the center is wearing a headdress with a large blue heart-shaped letter M—for Mary, perhaps, or for Merovingian, the "vine of Mary." The vine motif appears repeated in the background of each of the extant trumps of the Charles VI tarot deck, a further hint as to their hidden meaning.

Still standing at the table in the bookstore, fascinated by the book I was holding, I looked carefully at the cards pictured in turn, noting how each one fitted into the heresy. There the "Inquisition," the gigantic ogre-bully of the medieval world, trying to enslave the minds and spirits of the people with his enormous chain. This fifteenth trump, I discovered later, is usually called The Devil, but the obscene picture on this card is obviously a rendering of the male power principle unrestrained, gone berserk, enslaving the human community. The big ears of this disgusting figure probably represent the ubiquitous spies of the Inquisition, so eager to catch the merest whisper of heresy. No free-thinking person was safe during six hundred years of European history! I thought of those thousands imprisoned for their faith, those bound to stakes and burned alive. Throughout Western history the echo lingers: "Whatsoever you shall bind on earth shall be held bound . . ." What a legacy!

Another trump card indisputably associated with the heresy was the eighth, called Strength. The woman personifying this virtue holds the broken left pillar of the temple, a clear reference to the Davidic bloodline, disinherited and broken like the temple itself. Boaz, the husband of the widow Ruth, was the great-grandfather of King David, and the temple's left pillar was named Boaz in Hebrew (1 Kings 7:21).

Freemasonry, an offshoot of the Knights Templar, to this day retains in its rituals a lament for the "sons of the widow," an epithet for the royal bloodline of David, whose dynasty was to be established "in strength." The crippled king of the Grail legends is named "Anfortas," a lightly disguised corruption of the Latin *in fortis*, also meaning "in strength." This card's association of the broken pillar with the Davidic bloodline and the wounded king of the Grail is not accidental.

And the tarot trump called The Tower was particularly poignant in light of the historical suppression of the Grail family. Behind its image of the stricken tower was the lament of the royal heirs of David—the "vine" of Judah—expressed in Psalm 89, a dramatic litany of the broken promises of God to the House of David: "You have rejected and spurned . . . your anointed. You have renounced your covenant . . . and defiled his crown in the dust. You have broken down all his walls; you have laid his strongholds in ruins" (Psa. 89:39-41).

After the destruction of the Cathar strongholds and those of the Order of the Knights of the Temple, the titled families of the Languedoc must have been in deep despair, wondering why God's glorious promises for the restoration of the Holy City and the royal line of David had not come to pass. It is the heirs of Magdalene—both of her bloodline and of her Church of Amor—who are spurned, whose citadels are in ruins. I have visited the crumbled rocks of their medieval strongholds perched on pinnacles in southwestern France—Montsegur, Peyrepertuse, Queribus—bearing silent testimony to the ruthless tactics of the victorious allies, the French monarch and the pope. The powerful echo of the "Magdala"—the watchtower/stronghold—is also mirrored in this sixteenth tarot card.

After a few minutes studying the illustrations of the tarot trumps, I flipped to the text of the book in my hands. Its author suggested that while the cards were indicted by the Roman Catholic hierarchy as heretical, no one seemed to have had any idea what tenets of faith the cards were propagating. They remain an enigma in art.

Excited about my "chance" encounter with these cards, I wrote a short paper explaining the symbolism I had discovered in the tarot trumps. I called an art professor at Vanderbilt University and briefly explained to him that the medieval tarot trumps were the catechism for the heresy of the Holy Grail, offering to bring him a copy of the paper I had written. We made an appointment for the next day, and I visited with him and left my paper with him. I drove home, very excited about the discovery I had made and my conversation with the professor.

When I got home, I poured a cup of coffee for myself from my automatic coffeepot. It had been boiling away for several hours during my absence and had the consistency of syrup, but I did not even notice. I was totally caught up in my discovery of the secret of the tarot. I looked again at the first trump, The Fool, from one of the early decks pictured in my book. There was a skull lying on the ground, with holes in it. *I wonder what that pierced head is doing there?* I asked myself. And suddenly I knew! It represented Jesus' head, pierced by thorns. Perhaps it represented the skull rumored to have been brought to Europe by the Knights of the Temple.

I began to feel physically sick. Suppose the whole edifice of Christian doctrine was a house of cards? I was aghast. Suddenly it dawned on me that my discoveries had grave implications for the Church, and I broke out in a cold sweat. That ogre of the Middle Ages, the Inquisition, perhaps in some modern guise, might hunt me down, too. I was a heretic, just like those tortured and burned alive in the Middle Ages.

Heresy and truth are not mutually exclusive. Heresy is merely a belief at variance with the doctrines of the magisterium of the Church of Rome. But loyalty to the patriarchy was so strong in me, I began to be terrified of the consequences of my findings. I knew I had discovered the tragic flaw in Christianity. The strong patriarchal mold in which I was cast, the "faith of our fathers," had always insisted that to question the tenets of the Church was a deliberate affront to God. To break the mold of the patriarchs was a monolithic task! In my mind's eye, I saw an image of the blind folk hero Samson bringing down the temple of the Philistines, and I shook with apprehension.

What if the long arm of the Catholic Church decided to squelch me as it had others in the past? What would become of my children? I wondered. I had heard stories of police tactics behind the Iron Curtain and elsewhere. Many of our military friends stationed in foreign countries had to check their homes and automobiles several times a day for explosive devices. My fears now seem irrational, but at the time they were very real to me.

While my husband was away on a business trip that week, both of our younger sons were injured in their soccer games and both were now limping, one with a badly bruised thigh, the other with an injured knee. Watching them, I remembered the wounded king of the Grail legends. And the line "Bury my heart at Wounded Knee" began to flow through me like an electric current. I looked up "Wounded Knee" and read about the massacre of the Sioux Indians by the U.S. Cavalry. I was distraught. The military heritage of which I had been a proud and loyal daughter had clearly participated in an inglorious slaughter of Native Americans in that campaign. I wondered what other nasty surprises I would encounter if I questioned further. Everything I had once held sacred was proving to be flawed.

By now it was the December 12, the feast of Our Lady of Guadalupe—the dark Madonna of the red roses. In the middle of a sound sleep, I was suddenly awakened at 2:35 a.m. by the loud blaring of my clock radio. I had not set the alarm, but now, in the middle of the night, it was unexpectedly belting out a song I had never heard before. The words cut me to the heart: "Bury my heart in that old town, just bury my heart in that old town."

Perhaps Jesus was trying to get my attention, I mused, begging me to have his sacred wounded heart buried in the "old town," the town of the "wounded knee"—symbolic of the wounded masculine—so that the new era of balance and wholeness could begin. Our Emmanuel community had been specifically told years before that we, like the woman with the alabaster jar, were to anoint the body of Jesus for burial. I did not yet understand why Jesus needed to be buried, but I believed now that it was his wish. He was the sacrificed king, was he not? In order to be resurrected, he had first to be entombed.

In my confusion, I tried to understand the shattered pieces of the story I was trying to gather. God's heart was wounded, pierced like the side of Jesus with "Longinus," the long lance of the Roman centurion. My personal misery was intense. I tossed and turned in my bed, unable to sleep, my thoughts chasing one another around in circles. I wanted to help to heal the "wounded heart of God," but I did not know how. I did not yet fully understand the image of "the wounded knee"—the painful, masculine wound of the lonely king resulting from the loss of his partner.

On December 21, while dusting in my sons' room, I found myself thumbing through their *Golden Bible Atlas*, where I encountered a picture of a hexagram with a dove hovering over it. The text indicated that the symbol had been carved into the flagstone floor of the Fortress Antonio, where Jesus was believed to have been scourged and tormented by Roman soldiers, who first dressed him in purple and then crowned him with thorns.

I had already been shown the Sacred Marriage of the fire and water triangles, male and female, the archetypal symbol for the harmonious union of the opposites. But I had not until that day fully understood the visual image of wholeness—the six-pointed star— with the dove representing the presence of God hovering over the created cosmos. My friend Ann once told me that when the old age is dying, the sign of the new age is already present. I had not understood what she meant until this moment, staring down at the ✡ in my children's Bible atlas. Now I knew that the sign for the new age at the time of Christ was to have been the symbol of the Sacred Marriage. It had been lost or misunderstood for all this time. It was time to bring it back, because it was the symbol for peace and harmony as well as sacred union. Two thousand years had been wasted!

Suddenly I understood why the Cathars had so firmly refused to honor the cross; they saw it clearly as an instrument of torture. Jung's disciples have since explained that the symbol of the cross is unbalanced: the vertical "masculine" bar is greater in length than the horizontal "feminine" bar. The cross is a visual representation of orthodox Christianity, which (expressed in Jungian terms) values

Logos/reason more highly than Eros/relationship. It seemed to me that the cross was a visual image of the cultural imbalance of male and female and therefore, quite appropriately, a symbol for suffering.

That night when my husband returned from his trip, I tried to explain my insights to him. I told him that the hexagram with the dove brooding over it was the symbol that represented the harmonious and balanced forces of the cosmos. The ✡ was a model of wholeness and partnership, and the dove representing the Holy Spirit brooded over it with healing in its outstretched wings. I wanted to write to the pope to explain to him the importance of "sacred union" and the partnership symbol of the *hieros gamos*. The ✡, not the ✝, was the symbol inherent in the Gospels.

My husband was frankly appalled. All week I had been warning him about potential danger to our family from explosives and other imagined evils, and now I sprang on him this revelation about the hexagram replacing the cross. It was too bizarre for him! From any rational point of view, I had gone off the deep end.

The solid granite walls of my inner bastion were crumbling. Suddenly it was the dark night. Someone had lied! The "kingdom" could not come; it was built on a gigantic and fatal flaw. God was wounded. The Grail had been lost, Eros denied. The passionate woman—the Beloved—had been named Prostitute instead of Bride. God's heart was bleeding, pierced with the centurion's spear, Longinus.

Bleeding spear, bleeding cup; wounded male, wounded female; holy blood, holy grail . . . . The symbols finally overwhelmed me. I was having a nervous breakdown.

HARROWING HELL

When you pass through the water, I will be with you; in the rivers you shall not drown. When you walk through fire . . . the flames shall not consume you. (Isa. 43:2)

The account of this episode is acutely painful, but it is part of my journey and belongs in the record. Most people admitted to mental wards never fully recover. Many are kept sedated so that they will be "safe" and will not cause further embarrassment to their families. Or they are put on various mood-altering drugs that take away their "highs" and "lows" and change their personalities.

I have never read a specific account of what went through the head of someone who was having a nervous breakdown or of the intense and chaotic emotions they suffered. Such things are just not discussed. People prefer to pretend that nothing happened to them because the stigma of mental illness is so great. Some families are so upset and embarrassed that they do not even go to visit a family member who is hospitalized with a mental disorder. They are in a state of denial.

On the afternoon of December 22, my husband left me at the hospital for evaluation. I was shattered to the core, confused, and afraid. What terrified me most was the plight of my children in my absence. Who would take care of my four youngsters still at home, considering that my husband traveled out of town so often on business? Michael was only six and Edward, eight. Kate was in sixth grade and Meg in ninth. Dodd, who had always been my strong right arm, had left in June and was a plebe at West Point. He was home on leave for the Christmas holidays. They were aware that something was radically wrong with me. My driving had been affected by my mental state, and it had become increasingly difficult for me to provide meals on time or even to utter coherent thoughts. My distress for them was making me even more frantic.

Ten years later, looking back at the episode that occurred during the weeks of Advent in 1986, I realize that what I suffered was a spiritual crisis. Though I now know that it was a significant shortcut to my awakening, that does nothing to mitigate the pain I caused my family at the time. The grim reality was harrowing for us all. But my husband hoped that perhaps I could be helped by modern medicine. He helped me pack a bag and drove me to the hospital.

Coincidences that occurred during my hospital stay bordered on the bizarre. For someone in my anxiety-ridden state, they were excruciating, but perhaps for that very reason I remember them vividly. Throughout the ordeal, I had the feeling that some malevolent power wanted to discredit me as a witness or better yet, to incarcerate me for life on a mental ward. I made a conscious commitment that I would not allow fear to suck me into the abyss of insanity.

Tradition insists that Jesus went a docile victim to the slaughter prepared for him by the "establishment," the Roman government and collaborating Jewish priests. Perhaps by not being willing to be a docile victim, a sacrificial lamb led to slaughter, I failed some ultimate test. However, I remember that I made a conscious decision to survive and to return to a realm of reason and sanity. I would not succumb to the rough voice I kept hearing in my head, a deep, rasping voice that had been ordering me in harsh terms to perform various bizarre tasks, including calling an ambulance in the middle of the night or getting up at three o'clock in the morning to take a cold shower. I resisted the harsh, irrational dictates of this voice as hard as I could. Consciously and deliberately, I refused to obey its brusque commands, refused to cooperate. I would not give this authoritarian voice power over me. Consciously, I chose freedom.

For what seemed an interminable time, I sat in the waiting room of the psychiatry clinic in the huge hospital. Then the psychiatrist called me into his office. Standing in the corner of the room, near the window, was a large palm plant. A wooden crutch was, incongruously, standing upright in the pot, propped up against the plant.

I did a double take. *Why was there a crutch in a psychiatrist's office, resting against the stem of a large potted palm plant?* I wondered. In my mind, the crutch was an allusion to the wounded and crippled Bridegroom/King Jesus, bereft of his Bride, and the palm tree seemed symbolic of Israel and the royal house of David. I remembered that people spread palm branches before Jesus on his entry to Jerusalem, and called him Son of David. The palm tree is *phoenix* in Greek, like the mythical bird resurrected from the ashes. This bird, too, is a symbol for Christ.

Did the doctor know that? I wondered. Who had rested that crutch in the palm plant? And why? Was the psychiatrist conscious of all these symbols? Was he deliberately playing with the archetypes? Or was another power in control, programming the medical staff without their conscious knowledge? Perhaps the doctor did not even guess that he was being programmed? Was the crutch in the potted palm plant merely a "prop" in an unfolding drama?

Such questions streamed through my head. I was fearful. How could I find help in this place if the "enemy" was already in place here waiting for me, preparing the stage for the continuing drama that was going on inside my head, the battle for my mind and soul?

Hanging from the hook on the doctor's office door was a white fleecy jacket that looked like lambskin. *The lamb of the sacrifice,* I thought—*the martyr.* I recognized the jacket immediately. I owned one just like it and had worn it for years, unconsciously, thinking nothing of its symbolic meaning; it was just a nice warm woolly jacket. But what was a jacket exactly like mine doing hanging from a hook in the doctor's office? He was a military doctor and wore a dark green uniform to work. What possible use did *he* have for a fuzzy white "lambskin" jacket like mine? Perhaps it was another stage prop? And what about that crutch resting against the palm plant? It all seemed so bizarre.

These were not just delirious hallucinations running through my mind. The items were not imaginary. The only question was what they were doing in the psychiatrist's office! Several weeks later, on a follow-up visit and in a saner state, I returned to this office and deliberately looked for the crutch and the jacket. The crutch had been removed, but the jacket was still hanging on the peg on the office door. I recalled the story of the Babylonian goddess Inanna and her three days hanging on a meat hook in the underworld. Perhaps my descent into the underworld in some way paralleled hers.

I see now that, like Parzival, the poor fool in the Grail stories, I failed to ask the right questions at that first meeting with my doctor. I should have asked him what the crutch was doing in the plant and what the lambskin jacket was doing hanging on the hook on the door. I should have confronted him. But I was afraid. I did not want to tell him the whole story of what I knew because I feared his power to lock me up for good. So I deliberately gave vague answers to some of his questions, telling him only that I had made an important discovery in the tarot cards having to do with art and history, and that I had discovered a medieval heresy that would discredit the Church. Obviously this did not interest him.

After my preliminary evaluation by the psychiatrist, I was admitted to the hospital ward for intensive neurological testing. The doctor sent my husband home after first promising us both that I would be released on the third day, late in the afternoon of Christmas Eve.

What followed was a series of bizarre incidents that did nothing to soothe my agitation or mitigate my acute distress. One of the nurses on the ward wore orange lipstick on her top lip and purple on the bottom. It looked so weird, I couldn't believe that she was sincerely trying to help mental patients. The artwork on the wall near my bed was modern, discordant, and garish, in black and harsh shades of yellow. A nurse issued me a blue-and-white-striped bathrobe like that of the other patients on the ward, only mine was rumpled as if it had never been ironed and the strings were broken off, so the robe would not tie neatly. It was degrading. I wore my own black velour bathrobe under the issued garment, and I felt unbearably frumpy.

The other patients received medication and went to bed around 10 p.m. From the time of my admission on the ward, I had refused all medication because I did not want to obscure the results of the tests I was undergoing, and the doctor had concurred with my decision. I felt very vulnerable, as if I had been sold into an alien and hostile captivity.

Unable to sleep, I paced the halls for awhile after the other patients went to bed. There was no one visible on the ward although there was light, laughter, and cigarette smoke wafting from behind the door marked "Staff Only." From the lively voices, I presumed the night shift was relaxing, perhaps enjoying a Christmas party.

About 11:15, while I was walking around unsupervised in the halls of the ward, one of the nurses on the night shift came out into the hall wearing a long white lace negligee. She was very startled to see me. She started to giggle nervously, then tried to explain: She was getting married in a few weeks, and she was just modeling select items of her trousseau for her colleagues. *In the hall of a coed mental ward?* I asked myself. *In the middle of the night? Is she really a bride-to-be? Or is she insane?* Again I wondered if some unseen hand was orchestrating this whole crazy situation. It would make a good novel, I thought: Truth is stranger than fiction! I sought my room and eventually fell into a troubled sleep.

Looking back on my stay in the hospital, I realize that these three days, December 22 through 24, occur at the winter solstice, when the sun is at its lowest point of the year and the encroaching darkness looks as if it might take over. In my life, it almost did. Having so ardently served the masculine solar principle—the son/sun—all my life, I was now succumbing to powerful lunar influences unleashed by my nervous breakdown. The mitigating restraints of reason were absent and a bottomless pit of primeval chaos and insanity yawned before me.

The unsettling sequence of events continued. The day after my arrival at the hospital, I was scheduled for a CAT scan and had to be transferred by ambulance across town to another hospital where the test was to be done. I was still wearing the rumpled blue and white striped hospital robe with no strings, and although it was deep December and sleeting outside, no one bothered to offer me a coat. When I got into the ambulance, I saw that the passenger area was entirely bare, with benches along both the sides, but no seat belts. Once again I wondered whether the staff of this hospital really had all their marbles.

The ambulance driver was visibly distraught and looked as though she had been crying. We had two near wrecks on the way across town, with several irate drivers honking angrily at us from other vehicles. Our driver responded like a maniac, shifting in and out of lanes without signaling and swerving when angry drivers honked their horns. (I later learned that this was our young driver's first day behind the wheel of an ambulance; she had been very nervous about the trip because of the icy sleet on the streets and her inexperience at the wheel. No wonder she had been crying! I would not have been consoled by this information as I clung to the edge of my bench in the ambulance, praying decades of the rosary under my breath.)

At the other hospital I was dropped off in the radiology waiting room, where finally, after a wait of nearly two hours, the technician took me into the x-ray room. I was laid out on a table, strapped in so that I could not move, and then my head was moved into the x-ray machine, which looked like a white metal cave. The radiology technician told me the series of x-ray pictures would probably take fifteen or twenty minutes.

This is it, I remember thinking. My husband, who has a graduate degree in nuclear engineering, had always impressed upon me the danger of too much radiation and repeatedly warned me against allowing excessive dental or orthopedic x-rays for any of our children. *If some power really wants to render me harmless*, I thought, *all it has to do is to zap me now with too much radiation. Then I really will be totally "burned out!"* A holocaust indeed!

I lay strapped down in the nuclear machine, totally helpless and vulnerable. I was literally BOUND. I watched the clock, feeling as if I were on a special high-tech cross, a nuclear torture chamber custom designed for me. I was isolated, feeling helpless and entirely at the mercy of the technician who was conducting the CAT scan from the little cubicle next door.

I watched the minute hand creep around the perimeter of the clock on the wall. The scan took nearly fifty minutes rather than the fifteen I had been told to expect. The technician finally unstrapped me from the machine and sent me back to the waiting room to wait for the films to be developed so I could carry them to my doctor. The wait seemed interminable.

When I got back to the regular ward, I ate only a few saltines from a cellophane package and drank milk from a carton. The nurse in charge stopped me at the desk. "Don't eat anything that isn't sealed," she warned me, nodding her head slyly. I knew the staff nurses were supposed to spy on me, to watch my behavior and to report to the doctors, but it made me uncomfortable, just the same. The nurses seemed both hostile and cynical. I did not trust them. Until that moment, I had accepted their admonitions and demands docilely, trying to be cooperative.

Now, however, something inside me snapped. I confronted the nurse at the station, and I told her firmly that the bathrobe I had been given was missing its strings and was miserably wrinkled. I told her to see that I had a decent bathrobe if she expected me to wear the hospital garb—otherwise I would just wear my own robe. It is difficult to retain a modicum of self-respect in a mental ward, but I refused to look any worse than necessary. A few minutes later an orderly brought me a proper blue and white-striped hospital robe, ironed and with strings and a sash. I was astonished that my assertiveness had yielded an immediate positive result. Why had I not thought of it before?

Within the hour I was herded with the other patients on the ward to what they called "craft therapy." The attendant in the craft room directed me to choose a craft project—a macramé or paint-by-number kit. I told her I was leaving the next day and would not want to waste one of her craft kits. She should save it for someone else.

She smiled at me knowingly and patted me gently on the arm. "Lots of people think they are going to be allowed to get out of here," she said. "But they don't let them go. You'll probably be here for weeks, maybe even months, until there is an opening for you in the state mental hospital. If I were you, honey, I would pick a project."

I was silently appalled. I wondered if my doctor knew that members of his staff were telling me that I would not be going home on Christmas Eve as he had promised. Probably these people were only offering me their best guess, based on prior experience. They did not know that I had been promised that I would be home with my family for Christmas. Surely no doctor would break his word, I tried to assure myself.

Or would he? Now I was really angry! I was not then aware that anger is a positive stage in the process of psychological recovery I was undergoing, because I had not studied the process. I had been too busy studying medieval art and Church history. But I knew I was angry now! What right did the staff of a mental ward have to play games with its disturbed patients? What excuse did they have for issuing me a disreputable bathrobe? How could the nurses be permitted to wear weird, unmatched shades of lipstick, or to be deliberately rude to the patients, or to model their trousseau lingerie on the ward in the middle of the night? *Who was more disturbed—they or I?* I found myself asking.

Deeper questions of abuse and victimhood began to occur to me. How much does one suffer before asserting oneself? Must one collaborate with the oppressor? Don't we have a right at some point to just say "NO!" Perhaps it is more than a right. Perhaps we have an obligation to say "No" to the oppressors, those who would keep us in chains! Former first lady Nancy Reagan's admonition to our nation's youth regarding use of drugs was ringing in my ears: "Just say NO!" I felt my courage rising.

When our cohort of patients returned to the ward, there was a young girl mopping the corridor. She seemed intimidated, afraid to look at us because we were mental patients. She kept her eyes down as she mopped. She was wearing faded brown slacks and a tan shirt.

I remembered seeing her there also the day before. It seemed that her only task was to endlessly mop the linoleum corridors of the mental ward. A bright yellow "Wet Floor" sign was propped up in the area where she was working, and she used a bucket of filthy water to rinse her mop. The girl certainly appeared to be cast in the mode of Cinderella. I wondered fleetingly if she were another "prop" on the set at the ward. The entire episode seemed like a bad drama and the hospital staff and patients, mere actors on the stage.

Who had orchestrated this scenario? And to what purpose? It was like a nightmare, except that the events were actually occurring. I was conscious of every detail, so conscious that I was able later to write it all down in my journal.

That night, the evening of December 23, the staff on the ward played the movie *Ladyhawke* on the VCR in the patients' lounge. At first, it made me nervous. It was my favorite film, but I had not told them so. *Can they read my thoughts?* I wondered. How could they know so much about me? Eventually, I relaxed and found comfort watching the familiar scenes and the ultimate victory of Isabeau and Navarre over the evil bishop. In the final moments, the knight picks up his lady and holds her in the light. It lifted my spirits to see this ecstatic reunion of the lovers bathed in light as the sun emerged from the eclipse.

On the afternoon of Christmas Eve, my husband arrived to take me home. I had just returned from a neurological scan and I looked like an absolute freak. The technician had stuck little wires all over my head with some sort of sticky white putty that was now partially dried, and tufts of my hair were sticking out in all directions. The nurse instructed me to try to comb it out because, she insisted, I did not have time to wash my hair. I did not argue because I did not want to jeopardize or even postpone my departure. She was in charge—I was only an inmate. My husband looked horrified when he saw me, but made no comment. He should have been warmly commended for his self-restraint!

The chief psychiatrist invited us to come into his office. The Cinderella woman-child was still (or again?) swabbing the hall with her dirty mop, and the corridor floor was glistening wet. The doctor paused at the threshold of his office. Then, inexplicably, he stooped down on one knee and patted the floor. He glanced up, gazing direct-ly at me, and said, "It's all right. It's almost dry."

I thought, not for the first time, that he must be truly bonkers! What was he doing kneeling at our feet, patting the floor? Perhaps he thought I was like the wicked old witch in the *Wizard of Oz*, who was afraid of water. I almost laughed!

I looked around the office as we entered. Incongruously, it was not an office at all, but a huge examining room, about twenty-five feet on each side. In the very center of the room, highlighted under a huge standing medical lamp, was an examining table with stirrups, like the ones in the gynecological clinic with which every mother of children is all too familiar. *Why was that lamp on, its unrelenting beam directed at the examining table, like the glaring lights in a theater?*

The table seemed a torture instrument, highlighted as it was in the center of the large room. It seemed to epitomize the universal suf-fering and degradation of women at their most vulnerable moment. Acutely, I felt their anguish and wretchedness— "wounded woman, bleeding grail." Perhaps this stirring of compassion for my sisters was a sign that my own wounded feminine was beginning to heal.

I thought of Jesus, nailed to the cross. He had submitted to the power of the ruling elite, who had decided that he was a threat to the establishment. He had been my role model for years: total submission to victimhood. "Just offer up your sufferings and disappointments," the nuns had taught us.

But now I was refusing to succumb to the power principle that seemed intent on destroying me. I was insisting on returning to the land of the living. I wanted wholeness, not martyrdom. I could not submit to being put away, perhaps to spend the rest of my life in a mental hospital—sacrificed to the void. I would insist on going home so that I could take what I had been shown and work to restore the Bride and to bring water to the desert, to help to cultivate the gar-den God had intended our world to be. I made a conscious decision that I would continue to serve, but not in chains! I would not allow anyone to extort from me, burning me out with incessant and insatiable demands, like those of Cinderella's stepsisters. I was not born into slavery but was a partner and cocreator with God.

My thinking crystallized into a new sense of personal empowerment. The people of Earth had been duped for centuries into believing that God wanted us to suffer patiently and docilely in the face of adversity, following in the footsteps of Christ. It was meant to be our lot, to test us and make us long for heaven. This mentality had allowed a few to have power over the many and kept us from taking responsibility for our own wholeness and well-being. We had been called "children," instead of partners. From now on I would set my own goals and standards. I would climb down from the Logos-oriented cross and redesign my life based on the blueprint for balance and wholeness, the ✡ I had been shown.

I tried to focus on the conversation my husband was having with the doctor, who was discussing the drug he was prescribing for me. During the three days of testing, he had found no evidence of a brain tumor or organic problem, so he had decided that my "episode" was due to an emotional disorder. The medicine was new, he told us, and might have a few disturbing side effects. For example, it might cause me to lactate.

My husband nodded, assuring the doctor that he understood. Both of them were acting as if I were not even in the room. Of course, they could not look at me with any degree of comfort because my hair was sticking out all over my head in weird tufts from the sticky white putty.

"She might develop a twitch or a tic," the doctor continued. He then demonstrated what he meant, allowing his arm to jerk at his side every few seconds. Then he did it with his face and neck, jerking his head—in a ghastly pantomime. He was a very clever mimic! I might have laughed at his simulation, except that it was not funny. I glanced at my husband. He was watching the doctor intently. In horror, I realized that he might even consider letting me take that medicine.

The doctor was continuing: "Her eyes might start to roll back in their sockets." He demonstrated. "If it gets too bad, you must give her an antidote."

My husband was still watching the doctor intently. I thought of the weeks on end when business took him out of town, leaving me to cope alone with the needs of our children. What does "too bad" mean? How bad is "too bad?" I wondered who would administer the antidote—who would be there to determine if it were needed? My fourteen-year-old daughter, perhaps? Or would it be my eleven-year-old? I shuddered.

The doctor went on with his instructions. He wanted me to consider getting a part-time job so I would not spend so much time "idly sitting around the house" alone. Now I almost laughed out loud. I had not sat down for years except to do research, and that was usually after 10 p.m. at night, when everyone else was asleep. I never had time to read novels. I spent my waking hours cleaning, cooking, doing laundry and errands and dishes, hauling groceries, endlessly chauffeuring children to soccer and basketball practice or cub scouts or church or the library, to doctors and orthodontists. Later I read what the psychiatrist had written in my medical file: that I was the mother of "two grown children." So much for his ability to remember details gleaned during an interview. I wonder what else he thought he knew about me!

I have since learned that barely one-fourth of mentally ill patients are ever restored to normal functioning after their combination of "therapy" and medication. No wonder, if their therapy and medication were anything like those I was in danger of receiving!

On our way home I told my husband that there was no way I would take the medicine the doctor had prescribed. He looked visibly relieved. He, too, had been horrified by the doctor's description of the possible side effects of the new drug. We shared a deep skepticism about the use of mood-altering drugs in my case. I wanted a period of time to get myself back together without any medication. After three days on the mental ward, I was truly convinced that I was at least as sane as the staff on the ward, and maybe more so. I was waking up at last!

All I needed was a good home-cooked meal and hugs from those I loved.

I believe now that this experience of Advent 1986, from start to finish, was an important part of my awakening. The doctors and hospital staff seemed to have been programmed like actors on a stage, speaking their lines so as to trigger my transformation. Their script managed to jolt me into looking at reality.

All my life I had been taught to do what was expected of me, to accept adversity, taking it lying down, patiently enduring and accepting events without balking or complaining or rocking the boat. When I saw the girl with the bucket and mop, endlessly scrubbing the corridors on the mental ward, I was seeing a mirror image of my own role as Cinderella, relegated to menial chores. I had always expected to pour myself out in service to others, this being the model for holiness in Christianity and the lot of mothers on our planet. I shuddered involuntarily. Service is an important "way" to enlightenment, but abject subservience spawns the beast in others, who then easily take advantage of those willing to serve.

My spiritual and emotional crisis had occurred at the winter solstice, when the sun is at its lowest point of the year and the deepening dark of night looks as if it might take over. It had coincided also with a full moon, and I spent exactly three days in the "underworld"—a seething cauldron of insanity, my thoughts and emotions chasing one another around in an endless race, leaping from one non sequitur to another. Everything I had encountered in the hospital had seemed to have symbolic meaning for me, seemed to be trying to teach me something about the workings of the human mind and its partner psyche—about the intimate interconnectedness of body, emotions, mind, and spirit.

Something powerful and deep has existed in the human psyche from time immemorial that panics when the sun's light gradually recedes day by day. The festivals held at the winter solstice in every culture since time before time are designed to pray for its return, to coax it back, and to celebrate its rebirth.

However, my descent into an inner darkness at the time of the winter solstice was actually a powerful time of new awareness. As I now look back, I realize that I discovered things that Christmas about the workings of the human psyche, about psychology and symbolism, and about the interchangeability of mind and matter that I could never have learned in any other way. It was as if the encounter with the naked contents of my own unconscious were a necessary shortcut through the dark forests of the unknown, without which I would not have been prepared to receive the enlightenment that followed.

In the process of my transition, I was not less conscious; I was superconscious, accessing ways of knowing that were not in my usual mode. Synchronicities were pouring through me, showing me connections I could never have imagined. And I was given the gift of interpreting the symbols and the knowledge that I did not have to accept anything as final, but rather had the power to rewrite the script to suit myself. It was as if I had been given antennae with which to pick up information from unsuspected frequencies. My spiritual crisis was like that of a butterfly bursting its cocoon to enter a new phase. But at the time I had no inkling of the process of transformation that was occurring. It was an uncharted sea!

My task when I gradually returned to my normal conscious state was to sort through the events I had experienced and to make sense of them—to discover their meaning and purpose. Luckily, my friend Ann Requa had suggested months before that I begin to journal, and I now used this tool to help with my "alchemical" process of healing.

When I got home, I hugged my children and then took a shower to wash the putty out of my hair. We cooked a late dinner and then opened a large package that had arrived from my mother-in-law containing lots of small gifts for the children's stockings. I baked blueberry muffins for breakfast on Christmas morning. I had not bought anything much for Christmas, but we managed to celebrate with the generous presents others had sent.

On Christmas afternoon, I went out in the yard to plant some bulbs I had meant to put in the ground in early December before I got so distracted. Somehow, it felt therapeutic to kneel on the cold, dark ground and dig in the earth. Carefully, I placed the tulip and daffodil bulbs in the holes I had dug and covered them up. I was deliberately and consciously planting hope.

Over the next weeks, I took one task at a time, one day at a time. I could not read at first, because I could not concentrate. I focused on the mundane—on eating proper meals and spending time outdoors when it was warm enough to take a walk or work in the garden. And I hugged my children closer than ever. A week or so after Christmas, I called Mary Beben and Ann Requa to tell them the story of my incarceration, receiving their encouragement and advice. I wrote regularly in my journal, reconstructing the events that had led up to my breakdown and the things that had happened in the hospital.

My whole belief system, relied upon since earliest childhood, had been shattered. I recalled the prophecy from the snowy night of the *Challenger* disaster, January 28, 1986: "Fallen is Babylon, and all the images of her gods are smashed to the ground." Deeply I mourned my "Babylon," the patriarchal Church of my youth and its powerful male image of God so long entrenched in my psyche, now lying in rubble. I had felt secure in the old system, knowing my place, assured of my salvation. But now I was a pioneer, an explorer of unmapped territory, uncharted waters. I had no light except my total trust in Christ and the Holy Spirit.

The giant flaw in the foundation upon which Christianity is built is gradually being exposed now as archaeologists, Scripture scholars, and theologians reexamine history. Daily they discover more conclusive evidence that the Roman Catholic Church was built on the authoritarian model of Roman imperial administration, not on the blueprint of a Gospel of reconciliation revealed by Jesus. The formidable institution called "the Church" was based on former patriarchal religions and their worship of a sun-god principle with all its trappings of power and glory, might and dominion. It was shepherded by a privileged priesthood reluctant to share power or responsibility. A small hierarchy of ordained priests had complete control of the decisions within its walls.

These men also maintained a major father image in our minds and hearts, strengthened with centuries of tradition. They provided structure and security, and we were assured that we could rely on them and trust them. How could they be wrong? Were they not God's chosen authority?

The Roman Catholic Church claims that its priests and prelates are ordained in the footsteps of the apostles in an unbroken line—the "apostolic succession," as it is called. They and the altars they served are declared holy, set apart. They came to resemble the privileged god-kings of the pagan temples, like those of Egypt and Babylon. And the Jesus they enthroned at the "right hand of the Father" was an idol, like the pagan Baal of the ancient Middle East with his epithets of "lord and master," who taught the people worship of the solar attributes of power and dominion. The exalted male principle is an idol that turns the garden of God into a shriveled wasteland.

Yes, it is an idol. But it is an idol we have known and loved. We have depended on it and on the fathers who gave it life. It is deeply embedded in our psyche—both communal and individual. With its emphasis on reason, law, and order, the solar principle has formed and guided our civilization for two thousand years and more!

During the months of 1986, the new revelation we received destroyed the authoritarian, strong-man father image, turning it to ashes. The monolithic ecclesiastical structure that had sheltered us and on which we had depended had been razed, and there was nothing yet to replace it. But my closest friends and I had not lost our faith. We were only being purified and healed of toxic illusions. Over a period of several years, we had been shown how to reject and repudiate the false images that had been placed upon God. The time had come to purify our understanding of "the Holy One," to cleanse the altars of our hearts so long defiled by idolatrous "sun" worship.

This purification was shocking and painful because of many layers of reality built upon our long-beloved "father image" of God, like Michelangelo's painting on the ceiling of the Sistine Chapel. I grieved for my lost security—but the process eventually led me through devastation, out of bondage, and into a new freedom. I no longer relied so heavily on the traditional practices of my Roman Catholic heritage with its rules and punishments, but had a new confidence in my own intuitive impulses. Gradually I was learning to look inward for the authority to speak and to feel. Emotions I had repressed for years were not "irrelevant" anymore. They mattered because they mattered *to me*! On a day-to-day basis, I developed an even greater trust in the Holy Spirit—the Alpha and the Omega! And when I shared these thoughts with several of my Emmanuel sisters, they understood and told me they were experiencing a similar process.

The symbol for wholeness I now embrace is one of neither matriarchy nor patriarchy, but rather a "Godde"-centered, holistic partnership at all levels. (This creative new spelling of God represents the "sacred union" and is designed to include both masculine and feminine attributes of the Divine.) We do not seek to banish the masculine principle or injure it further; it is suffering intensely already. It just does not understand that it is severely wounded by the lack—even the denial—of its feminine counterpart.

Hopefully our civilization will not seek now to devalue the masculine as the feminine has been devalued. That would only create a noxious swamp where the desert once was! We continue to pray for the current patriarchs of the Christian faith, that while they still retain some authority and credibility, they will admit the grievous fault of two millennia, the distortion of truth. They could now lead us all to embrace together the neglected feminine side of God and humbly face the truth before it dawns too suddenly upon the world.

I covered much unmapped terrain during my journey into the depths of my unconscious. Perhaps when others hear my story and that of numerous "holocaust" survivors who have suffered a similar "burnout" and subsequent awakening, some can be spared the intense trauma of the collapse of the patriarchal paradigm. At least they will have the benefit of knowing that others have survived the harrowing of fire and flood and have found healing. Perhaps they can take encouragement from the experiences related here. As on the burned-out slopes of Mount Saint Helens, new life is gradually emerging, blooming and flourishing, a sign of renewal and hope for future generations.

CHAPTER IX

MAGDALENE'S LEGACY

. . . and when you hear the trumpet, listen! (Isa. 18:3b)

My release from the hospital on Christmas Eve had allowed me to rejoin my family. I felt safe at home again, but only very gradually did I learn to fully trust in the message that was seeking me through synchronicity, trying to find a voice willing to proclaim it. At first I was very reluctant to pursue my interest in the Grail heresy, but little by little over the months, I found the strength to continue the search. I was still curious as to how the medieval legends of Mary Magdalene in France might be related to numerous images of the Black Madonna in southern-European shrines. Why did I have a nagging feeling that there was a possible connection? I wondered. And then I experienced an encounter that illuminated the whole question like a blazing torch.

One day in June, in a fit of total frustration, I finally told Jesus that I just could not carry my quest for the Black Madonna and the Holy Grail one step further. It was swallowing up my days and giving me no rest. Whenever I asked a priest or a friend to confront the issue with me, I met with rebuff. No one wanted to hear about the secrets of the Holy Grail.

Of my Emmanuel friends, only Mary Beben knew the whole Grail story I had shared with her and even she was uncomfortable about it, especially after my nervous breakdown. I was fearful of continuing on my own, fearful of the isolation I felt, fearful for my own fragile equilibrium. I did not want to be a heretic, out on a limb by myself—scorned and shunned. It was making my whole family acutely uncomfortable in addition to the inner turmoil it was causing in me!

On this particular sunny Saturday afternoon, while driving my children home from a baseball game, I silently told Jesus that I was washing my hands of the Holy Grail. I asked him please to take the Grail back and put it on a shelf until he found some one strong and brave enough to handle it. Unless he did something radical to reaffirm my quest and to assure me that he was with me, helping me in my quest for the truth, he would just please choose someone else to proclaim his lost Bride.

When I pulled the van full of children into the driveway, my husband met me at the door. He had forgotten to tell me that we were expected to have dinner with a large group visiting Nashville on official business. His office had set up their itinerary, and they had responded by inviting us to enjoy a farewell dinner with them. I donned a dress and put supper on the table for the children on my way out the door.

During my husband's three-year assignment in Nashville, this was the only time official visitors from out-of-town had ever invited us to dinner. That in itself would have made the event significant, but in the car on our way to the Irish pub where we were to meet, Ted explained that our dinner companions that evening were French—mayors and deputy mayors from the *French Mediterranean coast* traveling on a working holiday with their wives. The foreign visitors were from Provence, and were serving on a committee that called itself (uncannily!) the "Syndicate of Waters." They were visiting Army Corps of Engineers dams that provided hydroelectric power, parks, and water-recreation sites in the United States, and they had somehow chosen Nashville for their interim destination en route to Disney World.

When Ted explained to me who the visitors were, I could hardly believe my ears! The fact that they were French was startling enough. But the name of their group was incredibly symbolic of the sacred feminine, so often associated with the element of water. Had they somehow been "sent?" My dinner companion turned out to be a delightful French woman, the wife of one of the deputy mayors on the Syndicate of Waters committee. She spoke little English, and I spoke virtually no French, but we had both done graduate study in Germany and spoke German at a similar level of fluency.

In response to my eager questions, Madame proceeded to tell me all about the shrines of the saints of the early Christian community at Les Saintes-Maries-de-la-Mer and the surrounding area near her home. When I asked specifically about the legends concerning Mary Magdalene and her family in Gaul, her face lit up with enthusiasm as she assured me unequivocally that they were all true! I did not tell her about the tenets of the Grail heresy—that Christ and Mary Magdalene were married and that their child survived—because in those days I was still very reluctant to share my suspicions about the flaw in the foundation of Christianity. Knowing the pain I had suffered in the breakdown of the patriarchal model in my own life, I was unwilling to cause others to question the "faith of our fathers." I was not yet ready to be responsible for the awakening of anyone else. I was having enough trouble with my own!

During the course of our conversation, my charming dinner partner told me all about the festival of the black Saint Sarah held during the last week of May every year in the seaside town where Mary Magdalene is said to have come ashore with Lazarus and Martha and their friends. My hair began to prickle at the back of my neck. I had not previously known about this festival, but the ritual, stemming from medieval times, revealed a long-standing folk memory of a "dark Madonna" image at home in the tiny coastal town on the French Mediterranean. For me, this dark image of the feminine had lingering echoes of the lost Bride, the widow of Sion, and other biblical images from the Hebrew Scriptures.

Madame, when I asked her, was not certain whether Mary Magdalene and Mary of Bethany were the same person, but her husband, sitting at her other side, confirmed that "la Madeleine" was the sister of Lazarus. I spent the entire evening taking mental notes of the lore and legends of Provence related by my companion. She seemed delighted as well as surprised to have found an American who shared her interest in Catholic shrines and the lives of the first-generation Christians who had settled in her homeland, and she shared with me every detail of that early community of saints that she could remember.

As the dinner was drawing to a close, the waiter who had been serving us all evening took off his apron and drew out a silver trumpet (only in Nashville!). We paused in our conversation, fascinated as the early notes wafted toward us: first the "Marseillaise" (the French National Anthem), followed by "The Star-Spangled Banner" and then, as a finale, "When the Saints Come Marching In."

Tears welled up in my eyes and streamed unbidden down my cheeks, even as I recalled the old adage about God having a sense of humor. I bent my head, trying to hide my face, and stared down at the napkin in my lap. It bore a green shamrock, Saint Patrick's symbol of the Holy Trinity, but an even older emblem of the Triple Goddess, the "three ladies" of Ireland. It was a poignant reminder of God's immanence: Wherever we are, GODDE IS.

After our dinner, the senior visiting dignitary, the mayor of the French Riviera town of Grimaud, presented my husband with a folder containing charming pen-and-ink sketches of landmarks from their homeland. One drawing was called "The Street of the Templars." Another sketch was of a chapel called "Our Lady of the Quest." A third showed a dark Madonna and a large "Grail" vessel. I shivered involuntarily as I was given these gifts straight from Provence. Only hours before, I had tried to give the Grail back to God, to be kept on a shelf for someone with more courage than I. Yet the portfolio of drawings had been packed more than a week before.

The silken threads behind the tapestry crisscross and are interconnected by the unseen hand of the Weaver. From that summer evening in the Irish pub in Nashville, I knew without a single shadow of doubt that I could never abandon the quest for the Grail or the mission to proclaim the Bride of Jesus. One of the lessons taught by the inscrutable Black Madonna is that Godde is a surprise: the *terra incognita*, an "unknown land." We cannot hope to wrap God up in a box with ribbon, like a birthday present. Enough times during the past several years I had heard the admonition of the prophet Isaiah (18:3): "All you who inhabit the world, who dwell on earth, when the signal is raised on the mountain, LOOK! When the trumpets blow, LISTEN!" (emphasis mine).

Years before, in 1980, I had seen the signal on the mountain, and now I had heard the trumpet, the call to action that I needed, giving me courage to proclaim aloud the story and the truth I had found so uncannily confirmed by unexpected coincidences.

Several weeks after the dinner engagement, my French dinner partner and her husband were so kind as to mail to me numerous booklets and pamphlets about the "Madeleine," guidebooks they had gathered from churches along the Mediterranean coast where they lived. Some of the pamphlets were in French, some in English, all with stories and pictures related to the legends I loved. Invariably these booklets referred to Marie Madeleine as the "sister of Lazarus."

I was overwhelmed by my French friends' spontaneous act of generosity. Sometimes I felt as if the whole cosmos were conspiring to help restore the Bride, like the little birds and mice in Disney's *Cinderella* movie who help the sooty-faced serving girl prepare for the dance. I now felt affirmed in my continuing quest to reclaim the lost Bride in the Christian story and the lost feminine in my own life. The fear I had felt in the hospital was fading, and my confidence growing from day to day as I pursued my research in the art and legends surrounding the Holy Grail.

There are several obvious possibilities with regard to the origins of the Grail heresy that circulated so widely in medieval Europe. It is always possible that it was contrived by enlightened ones—artists and alchemists—who wished to see the feminine principle restored to the paradigm of holiness and to human consciousness. Supporting evidence of legends, artifacts, and documents could have been manufactured by alchemists and occultists in a clever attempt to amend the orthodox tradition of the celibacy of Jesus, and the heresy might later have taken on a life of its own.

Considering that much of the extant evidence first appeared in the eleventh century and later, this might appear to be a viable conclusion. However, an oral tradition about the little family from Bethany and their companions in Provence appears to be much earlier.[1] And in Church tradition, all the way back to the second-century exegesis of Hippolytus of Rome and Origen, Magdalene is associated with the Beloved in the Canticle of Canticles: "dark and beautiful." She is the woman with the alabaster jar. There is only one important question yet to be answered: Was she prostitute or Bride?

This question has numerous levels of interpretation in light of the partnership paradigm of sacred union indigenous to Christianity. I believe it was the intent of Jesus, from the beginning of his ministry, to restore the feminine principle to a place of honor in a milieu that had become unbalanced and distorted under Roman hegemony in favor of masculine values of law, order, judgment, and power. The Gospels are full of admonitions attributed to Jesus: "Turn the other cheek"; "If he asks for your cloak, give him your shirt as well"; "Forgive seven-times-seventy times." Virtually every teaching of Christ has the same gentle, even "feminine," flavor as the Beatitudes from the Sermon on the Mount. One could easily conclude that Jesus desired to overturn the power-oriented value system of the Roman world exactly as he turned over the money changers' tables during the feast of Passover in the Temple.

The God whom Jesus knew did not insist on being worshiped with burnt offerings, but instead desired spiritual offerings of the heart: "I desire mercy and not sacrifice" (Hos. 6:6). God wanted to be loved like a bridegroom—like a bride. God wanted to nurture people like a mother, comfort them like a friend. God was not a jealous and angry potentate, but a passionate lover, desiring to be known and understood—to be loved, not feared.

The people, however, did not understand a loving God. They understood power. They understood winners and success stories: "To him who hath shall be given" (Mark 4:25). They were subjugated, exploited by their Roman conquerors, and they longed for a savior-messiah who could free them from the misery of their occupied nation and from Rome's tyranny, a savior who would judge their enemies harshly and punish them appropriately. Many did not want to be told that the Kingdom of God was already in their midst—in fact, within them!—or that it was only a matter of attitude adjustment, a matter of the heart, a matter of relying on one's own inner authority.

This was a lesson I, too, had needed to learn and was only gradually prepared to accept. Unlike border collies, who are bred to herd sheep, Christian "children" had been carefully trained to be herded, to remain under control, "within the walls," and to submit our reason to the external authority of the Church fathers, even when we were grown up, and even on such private issues as family size and the use of artificial birth control. Now I was learning to trust my own judgment in partnership with my own intuition and to trust my own conclusions, even though they might be at variance with the doctrines I had been taught in my youth and the catechism I had memorized in seventh grade at Saint Paul's Catholic School in the heart of Saint Petersburg, Florida.

When Jesus performed miracles, the people in the streets proclaimed him the Messiah. They wanted him to be their savior and lord. Scripture records: "And when Jesus saw that they would make him king, he fled to the mountain, himself alone" (John 6:15). When Peter saw him exalted and transfigured on the mountain and offered to build him a dwelling place there, Jesus said no.

But the successors of Peter ultimately built him a mountain-top kingdom anyhow, because many of his followers really wanted a "God of power and might" who could save them. Ultimately, they wanted a rigid set of rules they could obey and requirements they could fulfill, safe strong walls to protect them and a rock on which to stand.

For centuries Scripture readers have noted that Jesus was especially sympathetic toward women, generous with his time and attention to them. Seen in the perspective of the Roman Empire of the first century, the New Testament Gospels are remarkable in this respect, recording that Jesus accepted women as friends and companions. He preached a society where all were equal, where those who wished to be great must be great in their service to others, totally turning the tables of the hierarchical society, which had masters at the top and women, children, and slaves at the bottom—"bound on earth." Jesus preached and practiced an unprecedented equality of men and women, even to the extreme of allowing his Mary to sit at his feet in her home at Bethany, drinking in his words with the other disciples as if she were the most ardent of them all. And she was!

During several recent summers, I have returned to Europe to see what treasures I could find to corroborate my belief that people in the Middle Ages knew that Magdalene was the beloved wife of Jesus. Just walking in Provence has been a healing experience—feeling the Mediterranean sun on my face, seeing little wild flowers growing out of cracks in the walls of old houses, eating salads with chopped herbs and walnuts sprinkled on top.

I have also discovered widely scattered artworks that attest to interesting beliefs held in the Middle Ages about the enormous significance of Mary Magdalene. In altarpieces containing a group of statues gathered around the figure of Christ at his entombment, Mary Magdalene—"the great Mary"—is occasionally a full head taller than the other women at the scene.[2] In another interesting representation, she is wrapped in her hair at the center of a grouping of the twelve male apostles, again much taller than any of them.[3] Occasionally she is pictured, again wrapped in her glorious hair, being assumed into heaven, a doctrine hinting at the privileges of divinity usually reserved for the Blessed Mother, but commonly ascribed also to Magdalene in medieval legend. Some of these artworks survive in museums in France and Germany, others in out-of-the-way churches.

In the crypt of the cathedral at Metz in Lorraine in northeastern France I discovered an altarpiece where Mary Magdalene was clearly the "great Mary," larger than the others in the group. Metz was the seat of royal Merovingian power, and an eight-sided Templar chapel from the twelfth or thirteenth century still stands very near one of the oldest Christian churches in France, Saint Peter to the Nuns, whose decor included images of the vine and the Grail, twin pillars and equal-armed crosses carved in stone. Prominently displayed in the center of the Templar chapel itself is a large golden chalice— a "Grail" decorated with X's.

Honor of the Magdalene and her story must be deep-rooted in this city in the heart of Lorraine, I realized. I was stunned when I visited the treasure room of the cathedral there. Amid the jeweled croziers, monstrances, and vestments of the prelates were two paintings, both of Christ on the cross. In each painting there was only one other person in the scene: not his mother, not Saint John, but Mary Magdalene. She is shrouded in a red cloak, wrapped in despair, clinging to the cross. No other paintings are displayed among the cathedral treasures locked away and visited only by those willing to pay the entry price—only these two. *What do they know in Metz?* I wondered, as I gazed in awe at the paintings. *What do they remember that the rest of the Church has forgotten? Why do they consider these paintings so special that they are set apart, hidden from the people attending services, locked up at night? Do they intuit Magdalene as the Beloved?*

The Gospel of Philip found in the Nag Hammadi library of Coptic Scriptures claims that Mary Magdalene was the constant companion, the "consort" of the Savior, and the word used has specifically conjugal overtones.[4] Another ancient Gnostic text, the Gospel of Mary, states that the apostle Peter was jealous of Mary Magdalene because Jesus loved her best.[5]

This text mirrors the position of the official Church of Peter in the third and fourth centuries when the "fathers" succeeded in suppressing the influence of women, establishing an all-male hierarchy and proclaiming rigid rules in God's name. Peter's "rock" became a powerful monolithic institution, the strong right arm of the Roman emperor—a legalistic, "exoteric" Church—while the Gnostic tradition, the "esoteric" Church that honored the individual as a sacred container and instrument of the Holy Spirit, was deliberately swept aside. Yet, interestingly, it is this "feminine" tradition that somehow survived in Celtic Christian spirituality, a legacy that Coptic missionaries took to Ireland before their suppression in Egypt at the end of the fourth century.

A church dedicated to Mary Magdalene outside the walls of Jerusalem contains a painting of Peter seated on a thronelike chair. Mary Magdalene is kneeling at his feet, pleading with him. And he is pointing into the distance, clearly telling her to be gone. The painting seems to reflect the negative attitude of Peter toward Mary Magdalene expressed in the Gnostic Gospels. He was skeptical, judgmental, and jealous of Mary's intimacy with Christ, feelings that Peter's Church has maintained toward Gnostic traditions for centuries. What a shame this "Peter" could not have learned to love and to honor the "great Mary" as the Beloved of his Lord! But, late as it is, it is not too late. Perhaps "Peter" could yet have a change of heart!

The strongest possible statement in favor of monogamous marriage occurs in two canonical Gospels. Jesus is quoted: "And the two shall become one flesh. Therefore what God has joined together, let no man put asunder" (Mark 10:5; Matt. 19:6). What a terrible irony that Peter's Church, which does not recognize divorce of a man and woman whom God has joined in marriage, should have insisted all these years on the separation of Jesus and his Mary, with the resulting imbalances across the entire globe!

How can the "fathers" ever make restitution for their denial of Magdalene, for their having banished her as Abraham banished the bondwoman Hagar in the Book of Genesis! The wounds are severe and will not easily heal! How many marriages are aching for a model of true partnership? How many wives on our planet have been truly honored and their gifts cherished? When have we honored our deep emotions and treasured our bodies' profound wisdom? Have we celebrated equality and justice for *each individual* on the planet?

Magdalene's legacy has been too long denied, both in my own life and globally, where spouse and child abuse is rampant! How many mothers have tried to hide their initial disappointment when they learned that the child they brought forth was not a son? And how many single mothers have struggled to raise a child alone? For how many generations have we suffered the burden and excesses of male preferences, male choices, male abuses of power? Like the Bride in the Song of Solomon, Magdalene's daughters have poured out their lives, serving in the "sun" of their brothers' vineyards. No wonder icons of the Madonna weep in shrines around the world! Peter's Church needs to examine its position regarding the position of Mary Magdalene in light of the evidence from the Nag Hammadi Scriptures as well as its own. Direct evidence is there: She was the woman most revered in the Gospels, both canonical and Gnostic!

There is another Christian tradition that evolved in the twelfth century and existed side by side with the Church of Rome. This other church was called the Church of *Amor*, an anagram of *Roma*! It taught a "moist" or "green" tradition, a church of the heart, a church that believed that every person was a sacred container (a "Holy Grail"?) of the divine "spark" and could be filled with the Holy Spirit and enlightened by the Word of God.

The members of this "underground" Church of Love believed that God was immanent and imbued all creation, that this presence of God in all things could be encountered and savored in each soul. Its Scriptures were the New Testament Gospels translated into the vernacular, the "Langue d'oc," and its troubadours sang of the beauty of the Earth: the birds in the woods, the fragrant flowers of the meadows, and the joys of love and springtime.

The faithful charismatics of this hidden church were branded "Gnostics" because they believed that each believer could "know" God through direct, personal experience. They did not build large churches, but believed that all ground was sacred ground. Their tradition did not insist on the hierarchy of a privileged priesthood, but honored the sanctity of God's life incarnate in each human person, each earthen vessel, each sacred "grail." They lived their gospel of service to the *anawim*, a Hebrew word denoting the "little ones of God," trusting in the direct guidance of the Holy Spirit in every aspect of life.

This is the legacy of the hidden Church of Amor from the Middle Ages, so brutally suppressed by Rome's inquisitors. Those who discover and cherish this "other Church"—with its communion of the inner sanctuary—are Magdalene's true heirs! This is the tradition I have learned to love, the truth that resonated deeply within me, imbuing me with the courage to proclaim the story of the Lost Bride.

C H A P T E R   X

THE LORD OF THE FISHES

*And Jesus took the bread and gave it to them and likewise the fish.
(John 21:13)*

In 1988, the final year of my husband's tour of duty in Nashville,
I enrolled in classes at Vanderbilt Divinity School under a newly
initiated Master's in Theological Studies program made available
to lay people in the ecumenical community. Fascinated, I listened to
learned professors and Scripture scholars and pored over the readings
they assigned. I attended a course in the development and practice
of Rabbinic Judaism; one in the genre of the Apocalypse; one focused
on interpreting the Gospels; and another on the "New Testament as
Mythology." The opportunity was a great gift and these classes threw
more light on my spiritual path in my attempt to reclaim the forgotten feminine in Christianity. For several classes I wrote research
papers, including one about the connection between the anointing
of Jesus and the ancient rites of Sacred Marriage in the Near East and
another about the gematria encoded in the Book of Revelation, also
called the Apocalypse of John.

Continuing along the path of my spiritual quest, I discovered
convincing evidence that the new-age religion now called Christianity was an amalgam of the Jewish faith in the one true God and
traditions and beliefs of the Hellenized Roman Empire. The measurements of the New Jerusalem described in the Book of Revelation

confirm this theory of synthesis: a "marriage" combining Jewish traditions—the covenant of Moses, the exhortations of Hebrew prophets, and Jewish wisdom—with the astrological signs of the zodiac and mystery cults surrounding "savior" deities of the Greek/Roman pantheon.[1]

Contemplation of the canonical Christian Gospels coupled with my continuing research assures me that Jesus did not come to establish this new religion, but rather to fulfill the prophecies of the Jewish nation and to preach a new understanding of God's continuous presence with the community—the poor, the oppressed, and the disenfranchised—in the tradition of the Hebrew prophets. The Jesus portrayed in the Gospels was a charismatic Jewish teacher, healer, and prophet. He was a son of his people and the heir to God's vineyard Israel, an anti-establishment hero, infinitely compassionate toward the poor and the brokenhearted, and a champion for justice on their behalf.

The Jesus of Christian creeds formulated in later centuries is victor, ruler, and judge. He is the Son of God and Lord of the Universe; the second person of the Holy Trinity; only begotten and of one substance with the Father; ascended into heaven; and the object of Christian worship on Sunday. The Jesus Christ of institutionalized Christian tradition is a male solar divinity par excellence, portrayed in the oriental pattern of the sun gods of the Mediterranean world: Ra in Egypt, Apollo in Greece, Jupiter in Rome, and Sol Invictus in Constantinople. In Egypt, the pharaohs representing the authority of the sun god Ra were anointed with crocodile oil— the oil of the "beast" universally associated with the solar power principle—the "666."[2]

Then there is the other Jesus—the Jesus of the Gospels, a "historical" Jesus who was a gifted Jewish teacher from Galilee. This Jesus walked the dusty roads of Palestine in sandals, healed the sick, and embodied a radical, dynamic message of reconciliation, social justice, and service to others. He washed the feet of his companions, in spite of their protests. He was baptized under the sign of a dove (ancient totem of the Goddess),[3] anointed by a woman at Bethany, sentenced by the Roman procurator, and crucified as an insurrectionist. This Jesus fled whenever the people tried to proclaim him king and was nailed to a cross, a radical illustration of the woundedness of a holy God who is universally reviled, scorned, and tortured in the prophets who speak his word.

Parallel to the orthodox and canonical story of Christianity there is another story, a secret version of the life of Jesus, branded "heretical" by the Church and forced underground. In the shadow of the communities who came to believe in a "high" sun-oriented Christology of Jesus, the celestial and omnipotent king and "cloud-rider" who was expected to come in glory to establish his kingdom on Earth, there were communities of those who loved Jesus as brother and friend. These communities taught a simple gospel of spiritual transformation and believed that the Spirit filled not only the life of Jesus Christ, but *each* human life, imbuing it with holiness.

The "low" Christology of the first-century Ebionite Christians and later Arian heretics of the fourth through the sixth centuries in Western Europe shows a strong continuity with the original Jerusalem Christian community under the leadership of the James who was called the brother of Jesus. Their teachings insist on the true and full humanity of Jesus and his "sonship" as that of a chosen "vessel" committed to God's purposes, "a faithful servant"—faithful unto death—rather than the "Only Begotten Son of the Father" found in Christian creeds today.

Later Church fathers successfully transformed the Jewish Yeshua into an oriental potentate, over a period of centuries developing the high Christology officially articulated in the Nicene Creed (A.D. 325) that equated Jesus with God: "Light from light, true God from true God, begotten, not made, of one substance with the Father." On the way to this proclamation, the orthodox Church eventually (ironically!) labeled the Ebionites heretics and subsequently hounded the Arian Christians of Western Europe out of existence.

The doctrine of the true nature of Jesus is still being argued after two millennia. The bottom line of Christianity's current dilemma is the split between biblical scholarship and the doctrine of the divinity of Jesus, and the current rift between traditional conservative scholarship and some Bible scholars today often focuses on the question of the real human nature of Jesus. A deeper understanding of Jesus as "true man" and fully human in every way will ultimately transform the monolith of Christianity.

More potentially devastating for the Church than any political scandal, than any assassination, great though the fallout from those events, will be the spread of a revised understanding of *a fully human* Jesus—prophet and shaman, spirit-filled charismatic, itinerant teacher and miracle worker, true brother, true friend. He is at once an earthen vessel and a unique gift to the world—the Messiah, the Anointed One.

The ministry of Jesus shows a strong sense on his part that he was chosen to carry the message of God's passionate and inclusive love to his people. The epithets and cult trappings of pagan sun gods were later ascribed to Jesus by the Hellenist residents of the Roman Empire, who recognized the mythic dimensions in the story of the crucified king of the Jews. The message and life of the real Jesus were, after his death, deliberately packaged by Saint Paul and other missionaries to appeal to the Gentiles of the Mediterranean Basin, to bring to them the "Good News" of the Risen Christ and his message.

Surely the intelligentsia of the Roman Empire recognized in the "Risen Lord" of the Christians the sacrificed archetypal Shepherd/King and Bridegroom of the ancient pagan fertility cults. The Christian Scriptures confirmed Jesus as *Kyrios*—the Greek word identifying the "bearer" or the "lord of the age." The cult of the "sacrificed Bridegroom/King," mingled with the sun-god images of the Greek god Apollo and the Roman Sol Invictus in the melting pot of the Roman Empire, accounts for many of the doctrines, rituals, and practices of the early Christians.

I do not believe, however, that the real historical Jesus ever intended or wished to be worshiped as the supreme lord and master of the universe. The new religion later formed around his memory was adopted by the patriarchal power structure that eventually institutionalized the good news of his ministry on Earth and sacrificial death on the cross. The historical Jesus of Nazareth, called "Rabbi" (teacher) by his disciples, would have been appalled!

Early in my research, I noticed the motif of the fishes so prevalent in the Gospel stories, where the apostles of Jesus were called to be "fishers of men"; it was so widespread, no one could miss it! Mark's Gospel, the first one written, mentions the feeding of the multitudes with the five barley loaves and two fishes, and the other three Gospels include a similar story. Tertullian (A.D. 155-200) and Clement of Alexandria (A.D. 150-215) both used the fish as an appropriate symbol for Jesus, and Saint Augustine perpetuated the practice. Early Christian homilists referred to their parishioners as *pisciculi*, the "little fishes," and the baptismal font was called the *piscina*, the "fish pond."[4]

Yet with all these references to fish, none of them were associated directly with Jesus, I realized. I found it intriguing that in the canonical Gospels the actual epithets of Jesus—gleaned to some degree from the phrases he himself had spoken—include Good Shepherd, Bridegroom, and "heir of the vineyard." And names assigned to him by others include Rabbi, Messiah, Lamb of God, and even Gardener. But he is never called "Fish." And never "Fisherman." However, the initials of the phrase "Jesus Christ, Son of God, Savior" were abbreviated by the early Christians to form the word ΙΧΘΥΣ (*Ichthys*) Greek for *fish*, and the members of the infant community are said to have drawn a fish in the sand as an identifying mark of their affiliation with the primitive Church.

Why all this emphasis on fishes? I wondered. *Was it only because fishing was a common livelihood in Galilee and Palestine?* My intuition, corroborated by research, insisted that it was not just that. It had to be seen in the larger context of the new sign of the zodiac rising: Pisces, the sign of the Fishes.

Christians today still use the identifying symbol of the fish, often displayed as a bumper sticker on their cars, but may not be aware that Jesus, their Lord, was consciously framed to be *Kyrios* of the astrological Age of Pisces dawning at the time of his birth. Study of the New Testament texts, particularly the Book of Revelation, assures me that their authors recognized Jesus as the lord of the new age. On purpose, they spelled his Hebrew name, Yeshua, in Greek letters Ιησους (*Ihsous*) so that the sum of the letters by their system of gematria would equal 888, the "fullness of eights."[5]

I had studied the Hellenistic practice of gematria so prevalent in the New Testament, a level of interpretation of the sacred texts that had later been abandoned. But it was still there, encoded in the original Greek of the Gospels. The subject had fascinated me ever since my first encounter with gematria in John Michell's book, *The City of Revelation*, in 1971, soon after my own spiritual awakening to the Christian way.

In the classical system of sacred geometry, the number 8 signified regeneration, rebirth, and the dawn of a "new day," based on the beginning of a new cycle following the seventh—and last—day of a week. The gematria of the Greek word *Kyrios* is 800. The *Kyrios* was the lord of the new era, bearer of the new cultural thrust and the new paradigm. Both numbers—800 and 888—represented the idea of renewal and resurrection inherent in the number 8. And both were intentionally associated with Jesus Christ.

When I sought evidence that the dawn of Pisces was a strong influence on the authors of Christianity, I found numerous confirmations. Two fish drawn together—the astrological sign of Pisces— are among the graffiti sketched on the walls of early Christian catacombs outside Rome. And from the beginning, the patriarchs often equated Jesus with the fish motif. When he multiplied the loaves and fishes to feed the "five thousand" in each of the four Gospels, it is stated specifically that *two* fishes were multiplied. Jesus was eventually appropriated by the Hellenist culture of the Mediterranean and raised as the *Kyrios* of Christianity, which was later to become the dominant Western religion of the Age of Pisces, the Fishes.

Resurrecting the male principle incarnate in Christ and enthroning it at the right hand of God in an external heaven ignored the cyclical nature of reality and the old mythologies dealing with the waxing and waning of the moon and the seasonal changes of the

Earth. In Western society, under the banner of Christianity, the solar principle reigns twenty-four hours a day for twelve months a year *in clear defiance of reality and of Earth's natural rhythms.* The worship of the Logos principle and an exclusively male image of God for two millennia has so distorted human society that it has ultimately endangered the fundamental balance of opposites necessary for life on our planet.

It is no wonder that in our highly industrialized society we are burning out the ozone layers, the rain forests, unique species of flora and fauna, and other irreplaceable resources, including perhaps even our brains! The prevailing paradigm "in heaven"—enthroned in our psyches—is the Δ, the "blade" or fire triangle that is the symbol for raw power, represented in the ancient world by the "yang" or solar number 666—the familiar "number of the beast" in the Book of Revelation.[6]

We should realize by now that the sun is not God; it is just another star, one of billions. And basking in its direct rays is known to be dangerous. Perhaps it is time to back away from our dangerous "sun" orientation and all that it implies! The historical Jesus, and his message of equality and brotherhood, of sharing and compassion, is for all ages and all times. His "way" of service to others is a path of purification and sanctity. Having attempted to pursue this path myself, I believe that his guidance and message are universally valid.

The legacy of Jesus will not be expunged as the Age of Pisces fades, but will continue to be honored and cherished along with that of other sages and saints—both women and men—who have been honored as prophets or incarnations of the eternal "Beloved." In studying Jesus and his teachings, "wise men seek him still." That is my favorite bumper-sticker slogan. Like the magi, we have seen his star. It is the star of wholeness, of partnership and harmony. It is the ancient blueprint for the cosmic temple, the ✡ representing the sacred union of the polarities.

As noted earlier in this chapter, the literary tradition surrounding Jesus is filled with allusions to fishermen: fishers of men; nets breaking; the loaves and fishes; the 153 fishes in the net; Peter the fisherman. All subsequent generations have associated Christianity with the fish. In the idiom of the first century, the astrological Age of Aries (the Ram) had been superseded by that of Jesus Christ, the Lord of the Fishes.

My research suggests that during the course of the decades following his crucifixion, Jesus Christ was consciously adopted by the Roman Empire to be the bridge between the dying and rising astrological ages named for the constellations of the zodiac. The passing of the Age of the Ram seems to be significantly represented by the frequent New Testament references to Jesus as the Lamb of God, with its connotations of ultimate sacrifice. His crucifixion as the slaughtered lamb was viewed esoterically as the culmination of the dying age, the death of Aries, and his resurrection as the "Christ" constituted the birth of the new. Mithraism, a strong solar cult of the Roman Empire, had celebrated the precession of the signs of the zodiac with rites honoring the death of the Bull—the Age of Taurus. That widespread religion popular with Rome's legions was gradually superseded by Christianity and its lord, understood to embody both the sacrificed Lamb of Aries and the rising Fish of Pisces.

After the death of Jesus, the Lamb of God, pious Jews continued to make their offerings of lambs and turtledoves for only four more decades before the final destruction of their Temple and the cult of animal sacrifice practiced there. With the destruction of the Temple of Jerusalem in A.D. 70, the practice of offering animal holocausts demanded by Jewish law was irrevocably terminated. In occult terminology, the Age of Aries was officially over; the Age of Pisces had already begun—in a garden at dawn on that first Easter morning.

Since the early years of my quest for truth and my interest in the numbers encoded in the New Testament, I have been fascinated by the lore surrounding the meanings of the numerical values of the sacred canon—their antiquity and their symbolism. For example, the Hebrew Scriptures were clearly designed around the mystical number 7, the traditional culmination of a week—the Sabbath day when God rested from his creative work.

For the Christian community of the New Covenant, however, the number 8 was of paramount importance. Because it follows the 7 denoting the end of a cycle, 8 is the number of the rebirth and denotes the beginning of a new cycle—the "new day" or "new age." We have already discussed the use of this 8 in the Greek spelling of the name and title of Jesus. His resurrection occurred on the "eighth day," the day following the Sabbath—symbolically: the "sunrise" or "dawn of the new day" or the "age to come."

In the historical person Jesus of Nazareth, the initiated "who had eyes to see" discovered that the archetypal myth of the dying and rising god, a personification of the cosmic principle of regeneration, had taken flesh. The resurrection of the Savior Son was reflected in the encoded 888 of the holy name Iησους at which, according to Saint Paul, "every knee should bend" (Phil. 2:10).

New wineskins were needed to contain the cultural thrust for the ideals of the dawning the Age of Pisces, so someone had to articulate a new system. It may be impossible now to figure out who it was who first recognized Jesus as the long-awaited Kyrios or who first identified Jesus as Iχθυς (Ichthys) and Lord of the Fishes and packaged this message for mass consumption in the vast reaches of the Roman Empire.

One plausible explanation is that it was the work of esoteric mystery school initiates in the early centuries of Christianity who contrived a system of doctrine to give continuity to the underlying values of their civilization.[7] Chaotic social changes and cross-pollination of cultures (very similar to those of our current era!) created unprecedented turmoil during the early centuries of Christianity. The citizens of the Roman Empire, steeped in astrology and acutely aware of the movements of the zodiac, were seeking a focal point for the rising constellation of the Fishes, an avatar to proclaim a new cultural direction. The story of the Magi, wise astrologers who followed the star in search of the newborn king (Matt. 2), illustrates this point.

The emperors of Rome who claimed to be deities and insisted on being worshiped were not the long-awaited messiah. They were often feared and hated by the repressed peoples in the outlying provinces of their empire. The apocalyptic literature found among the intertestamental writings attests to the miseries suffered by the conquered citizens of Rome's provinces, who longed for salvation and retribution. The authors of the New Testament writings, Saint Paul, and perhaps even Jesus himself, seem to have expected the world as they knew it to come to an imminent and violent end.

Fear was the under-girding emotion of their day-to-day suffering, spawned by cataclysmic events that were recorded during the first century: disastrous droughts and famines, cataclysmic volcanic eruptions and earthquakes. Many in the Roman Empire believed that their civilization was crumbling, while others believed that it would continue but in a drastically revised form. These deep-seated fears of the community are reflected in numerous apocalyptic works of the period and in the Gospels of Christianity, culminating in the prophecy of Jesus that the stones of the Temple would not be left one on top of the other (Mark 13:2).

When their Temple in Jerusalem was actually destroyed and its walls torn down on the 9th of Av in A.D. 70, the residents of Jerusalem must have felt especial horror because that ultimate disaster occurred on the exact anniversary of its earlier destruction by the Babylonian armies of Nebuchadnezzar in 586 B.C. The embryo community of Christians in Jerusalem did not survive the destruction of the Holy City. As they and their neighbors fled for their lives to the outlying hills, they must have felt that the wrath of God was well and truly being visited upon them!

New Testament phrases coded by gematria tie into the sacred numbers of the ancient cosmology and were intentionally coined to adapt the Jewish messianic martyr Jesus to the framework of existing religious beliefs in the Mediterranean region. In the mystery religions of the Hellenistic world, mystical regeneration by means of sacramental participation in the death and sacrifice of a redeemer god was already practiced in the cults of Osiris, Tammuz, Adonis, and Dionysus. Many elements of early Christian doctrine and liturgy, particularly the cultic "thanksgiving" or eucharistic meal and baptismal purification rites, can be interpreted as an attempt to reconcile and adapt the teachings of the historical Jesus, the "Son of God," into religious rites borrowed from the mystery cults of savior gods popular in the Roman Empire. At eucharistic meals of the early Christians, fish was eaten in addition to the bread and wine common to several other cultic meals.

Establishing Jesus as "Lord," finally superseding even the Roman Emperor, took several centuries, but eventually Jesus was proclaimed throughout the empire as *Kyrios*, symbolically seated on a celestial throne at God's right hand.

One day in the spring of 1990 I was dwelling on Jesus as lord of the prophesied "age to come" and how his message of equality, justice, and service had been distorted. My thoughts drifted to comments Mary Beben had made during a telephone conversation a few days before. She had felt moved to set her goldfish free in a stream near her house in Virginia after noticing that the goldfish seemed lonely and isolated in its little glass bowl. She had decided it needed to be set free from its solitary confinement and allowed to mingle with other fish in the great outdoors. As I reflected on Mary's goldfish, I became aware of Christ, the singular *Ichthys* of Christianity, and wondered if he, too, were lonely.

I opened my Bible, because I often prayed with Scripture, and looked down at the passage on the open page before me, familiar lines from the Book of Job: "Perish the day on which I was born," I read, "the night when they declared 'the child is a boy'" (3:1). Now, even as I read, the words of this lament of Job took a surprising twist. Suddenly the operative word was *boy* and Jesus himself, rather than Job, seemed to be uttering the lament, pleading that the entire "night"—the two millennia of the current age—might be erased, the "night" of Pisces when it was said that God's only child was *a boy!*

For in claiming that the divine child was male, the entire feminine half of creation had been devalued by implication. The lines from the lament of Job seemed to be expressing deep, even anguished, regret for the two thousand years of male ascendancy and the "double standard" perpetrated as a result of the declaration—later institutionalized!—"the child is a boy." In the dawning of the Age of Aquarius, the dark night of male dominance and patriarchal hegemony is almost over. But only if we are ready to allow it to be! For we are the hands and feet, the partners of Godde and the cocreators of the world in which we live. We have to be willing to hear Godde speak a new word, and to permit that new word to become flesh—in *us!*

My friend Mary and I have often discussed the bottom line of all we have learned. "If ever you got to Rome and had a chance to tell the pope and his cardinals what is amiss with the Catholic Church, what would you tell them?" she once asked me.

I answered that I would read to them aloud from the first chapter of Paul's letter to the Romans—very appropriately, since Paul was addressing the "Romans," too! In this important epistle he expounds on the fruits of idolatry: the devaluation of women, sexual perversion, avarice, malice, wickedness. The list is riveting, reflecting accurately a society that worships male primacy. It seems Holy Writ has been telling the "Romans" the same message for two millennia—that worship of an exclusively male image of God is destructive: "For while professing to be wise, they have become fools, and they have changed the glory of the incorruptible God for an image like unto corruptible man . . ." (Romans 1:22–23).

The text from Paul's letter to the Romans could not be any more explicit; a picture is worth a thousand words. In Christianity, the image of God incarnate in Jesus is distinctly, unquestionably masculine. Most of us have been convinced since earliest childhood that God is male, sadly warping the self-image and psyches of fully half the human race!

The means of this indoctrination have not been subtle. We have seen "God the Father" in paintings of God like those on the ceiling of the Sistine Chapel; we have seen pictures and statues of Jesus, and we have memorized the words of Christian creeds. Until very recently we have taken the masculinity of God totally for granted, unaware of the extent to which these male images and even male pronouns have distorted the consciousness of our entire civilization. Surely it is this orientation that Pope John Paul II desires to heal by suggesting that the Virgin Mary is the "Co-Redemptrix."

In the letter to the Romans, Saint Paul instructs the community about idolaters who make an image of God "like unto corruptible man." He admonishes, "Therefore God had given them up in the lustful desires of their heart to uncleanness so that they dishonor their own bodies among themselves, they who exchanged the truth of God for a lie and worshiped and served the creature rather than the creator" (Romans 1:24-25).

The appalling thing is that the prelates of the Church have never realized that Paul's words were addressed directly to *them*! It is *they* who for centuries have propagated a male-oriented religion and civilization based on the worship of an all-male Trinity and dictated by an all-male hierarchy. All around the world they have harvested the bitter fruits of that idolatry, warping the society that worships an anthropomorphic and visibly male image of God.

Yet these fathers of the Church have never thought of *themselves* as pagan. They have never thought to apply Paul's words to themselves, perhaps because they have not fully understood the metaphysical principle involved: "As above, so below." Nor have they contemplated the wisdom of the *hieros gamos*, the sacred model of *partnership*. The abuses and perversions on our planet are directly linked to false doctrines promoting the worship of the ascendant masculine principle: "When the sun always shines, there's a desert below." The lyrics of this old country hit echo through the years, along with the line that provides the practical antidote the song offers: "It takes a little rain to make a garden grow."

A NEW SONG

Sing to the Lord a new song . . . sing joyfully all you lands; break into song . . . (Psalm 98:1,4)

In July of 1988, Ted and I packed our four younger children into our old Ford van and headed west from Nashville across the Great Plains and over the Rocky Mountains and then across Washington state to a new military assignment at Fort Lewis, an hour's drive south of Seattle. Our new home was a beautiful, old Army post at the foot of Mount Rainier, the snow-capped volcano called "Tahoma" by Native Americans—a word meaning "mother of the waters." Huge Douglas fir trees line the parade field at Fort Lewis, framing the spectacular view of the mountain. And across the parade field from our red brick quarters was the Main Post Chapel.

Almost as soon as we unpacked our boxes, I was offered a job as the public relations coordinator for the forty-three chaplains assigned to the army division and corps headquarters stationed at Fort Lewis, a ministry to twenty thousand soldiers and their families. During the time I worked with the chaplains, I shared my newly discovered views about the forgotten Bride in Christianity with several of them.

In detail I discussed my revision of the Gospels and my story of Magdalene with a chaplain friend who was a Freemason and Southern Baptist minister. He was very open-minded and interested in my Grail research, and finally one day he admitted that he loved my revised interpretation of the Christian Gospel to include the wife of

Jesus. But, at the same time, he admitted that he was still reluctant to believe it because he had not received independent confirmation that it was true. Curious to know what form the confirmation he was seeking would take, I suggested that he pray for whatever assurance he needed.

The next morning my chaplain friend came to my office in great excitement. He had prayed for Scripture readings to confirm my research and had received Isaiah 43:14-20—verses explaining that the rescue of the captive exiles from Babylon will be even more marvelous than their escape from slavery in Egypt: "Remember not the past . . . see, I am doing something new . . . in the desert I make a way, in the wasteland rivers . . . I put water in the desert and rivers in the wasteland for my chosen people to drink."

But that was not all. Even as he marveled at the first text, he had asked for a second confirming passage and had opened his Bible to Matthew 26: the description of the anointing of Jesus at the banquet by the woman with the alabaster jar.

The readings my chaplain friend received had summed up the Sacred Marriage and the whole Grail promise to heal the wasteland, echoing the new song in my heart—the wedding song of the Beloveds! It is time. We must leave Babylon, the corrupt city of "sun/son"-worshipers, and find our way back to the Promised Land—the land of milk and honey where the sacred ✡ is the pattern for harmony and wholeness.

One day I was sitting in my kitchen having a cup of tea in the late afternoon before starting to cook supper. I was mulling over all I had learned about the lost feminine and wondering what to do with it. *What is it all for?* I wondered. *Is it just for me?* I glanced down at the table where my children had dropped their books when they came in from school. Lying on top was a book about the American abolitionist Harriet Tubman. Staring down at the book, I suddenly *knew* that what I had come to understand was not just for my own growth and edification. It was about setting prisoners free, and I would not rest until I had done my part in breaking the chains imposed on Western societies for centuries by the "Holy" Inquisition.

In my mind's eye, I saw the long line of the slaves on the underground railroad to freedom, singing their songs and following the "drinking gourd," the Big Dipper, as they headed north. Like Harriet Tubman, who returned to the South after she had won her own freedom and worked to help others to escape from slavery, my job would be to help make the waters of truth available by writing the story of the archetypal Bride. "You shall know the truth, and the truth shall make you free."

Suddenly I felt thirteen months pregnant with all the information I had studied, the insights I had been given. I sat down at the old Osborne computer that belonged to my children and began to type: "Chapter I—The Lost Bride" . . .

Several months later, the response of the senior Roman Catholic chaplain to the first draft of my manuscript was encouraging: "This could heal the Church!" My first publishing query was made to Bear & Company in *Santa Fe*; I loved the association with the "holy faith" because it was the holy faith of the earliest Christians that I was trying to reclaim along with the mandala of the Sacred Marriage that was to have been our birthright.

In 1993, following the publication of *The Woman with the Alabaster Jar*, I began traveling around the country giving lectures and signing books. For many years I had admired the work of British philosopher John Michell, and on a trip to the East Coast in October I met him at a convention in Washington, D.C. Dr. Michell was kind enough to talk with me about his work with gematria, expressing his disappointment that more people had not been interested in this tool for a deeper understanding of the Christian Scriptures.

That memorable afternoon I asked Dr. Michell if he had ever computed the gematria for Mary Magdalene. He told me he had not, and then, looking me straight in the eye, suggested that it might be *my* job. When I got back from my trip, I went straight to my Greek/English parallel Gospels to check the spelling and calculate Mary Magdalene's number. I was astounded! While the "888" of Ιησους (Jesus) was claimed by Saint Paul to be important beyond all other names, the coded number for Mary Magdalene is also incredibly and immensely significant.[1] How could it have been so casually overlooked for two entire millennia? Did *no one* care?

The Greek name Maria, adapted from the Hebrew Miriam, has a gematria value of 152, but the epithet η Μαγδαληνη (the Magdalene) bears the exact value of 153, the same number as "the fishes in the net" mentioned in the final chapter of John's Gospel. The apostles of Jesus were called to be "fishers of men" and symbolically, the "fishes" in their nets represented the community of believers, the *ekklesia*, the communal "Bride."[2]

I was even more ecstatic when my research in the months that followed revealed further dynamic dimensions of the number 153. Poring over information about mathematics developed by the Greeks and the sacred numbers of their cosmology, I discovered that 153 was one of the most significant values in the ancient canon of sacred geometry! The number 153 signified the square root of 3 and was specifically identified with the Vesica Piscis, the "almond" shape known as the "vessel" or "measure of the fish."[3] This () shape has specifically feminine associations and was known throughout the classical Hellenistic world as the *matrix*, the "mother," of all geometry. It was sometimes called the "vulva," and was even referred to as the "Holy of Holies" because of its feminine connotations of the "inner sanctum." Of all numbers in the ancient canon, the number 153 represented the Sacred Feminine—the Goddess in the Gospels.

Because of the leeway (known as the *colel*) of +1 or −1 allowed in the system of gematria, all the many Marias (gematria 152) in the New Testament can be identified with this symbol and its obvious feminine symbolism. But only the spelling of the epithet η Μαγδαληνη bears the exact "Goddess" number of the Vesica Piscis—153.

It is not possible that the spelling of the epithet applied to Mary Magdalene just accidentally added up to this all-important "Goddess" number, any more than the spelling of Ιησους (*Ihsous*) accidentally produced the number 888. The Greek spellings in the New Testament were deliberate, chosen because their gematria was so important to enhancement of the interpretation of the sacred texts.

But the revelation of the numbers did not end with the names of the two Beloveds. Another important discovery was disclosed. When the number 8 associated with Jesus Christ and the Resurrection is multiplied by the 153 of η Μαγδαληνη the resulting product is 1224: the gematria for the Greek word ιχθυες *(ichthyes)*, the "fishes." As the authors of Christianity designated Christ as the archetypal "Lord of the Fishes," the 1224 confirms that they must have understood Mary Magdalene to have been its Lady—he the Fish (Ιχθυs), she the "vessel of the fish," the (). The numbers encoded in the Gospels identified Christ and Magdalene *together* as the archetypal bearers of the "age to come."

The elegant numerical coding practiced by the Hellenistic authors of the New Testament is a treasure only now being appreciated after being hidden in darkness for millennia, ever since the Gospels were translated by Saint Jerome from Greek into Latin and the original numerical values of their gematria thereby obscured. But to those who now examine them, there can be not the least doubt that the Mary called the Magdalene was the Goddess hidden from the very beginning in the Christian Gospels!

Knowledge of this hidden wisdom has given me the confidence and the courage to proclaim her status in the early Christian community at workshops and lectures around the country. The numbers encoded in the Gospels themselves are direct evidence that confirms the Sacred Marriage at the heart of Christianity and the couple who formed the sacred mandala for the Age of Pisces, whose astrological symbol represents two fish swimming in opposite directions, similar to the yin/yang symbol of the Far East.

The song I am singing is a Song of Partnership—the wedding song of the Beloveds. But it is not a new song. It is a variation on a very old song. Its prototype is the Song of Songs.

There is a wonderful song in the musical version of *Les Misérables* that hints at the dawn of a new era of partnership. In the lyrics of "The Red and the Black," the passion Marius feels for his beautiful

Cosette is interwoven with the expectations of the students who are preparing to fight a revolution in the streets of Paris to bring about a better world. Marius laments, "Red, I feel my soul on fire; black, my world if she's not there; red, the color of desire; black, the color of despair." The other students present in the scene echo his metaphor: "Red, the blood of angry men, black, the dark of ages past; red, the day about to dawn; black, the night that ends at last!"

At the finale of the Broadway production of the musical, the entire cast sings of the dawn beyond the barricades of their revolution. In the 1980s, thunderous applause for the musical production of *Les Mis* echoed around the globe and shook the planet. In Nashville in 1989, on the night in April when my daughter Meg and I attended the production, it received a ten-minute standing ovation. Six months later, in the wake of the freedom movements in the countries behind the Iron Curtain, the Berlin Wall crumbled. The revolution is not yet over, but we are now becoming conscious of its direction and the democratic partnership model it seeks to make manifest.

Victor Hugo, the author of the nineteenth-century novel, was an Albigensian adherent of the Grail heresy, implicated as a grand master of the Priory of Sion, a secret society formed in the twelfth century to protect the Grail secret and, according to the authors of *Holy Blood, Holy Grail*, still extant.[4] Hugo's *Les Misérables* presages the dissolution of the "benevolent" but repressive patriarchy and the uncompromising legalism of the establishment. His hero, the ex-convict Jean Valjean, takes on the name Monsieur "Madeleine," while the name of the police-agent antagonist is "Javert," which means "I affirm" or "I establish." He clearly represents the rigid and unforgiving legalism of the establishment and its enforcers. The story ends with the marriage of Cosette and Marius, he a nobleman, she a prostitute's daughter. At the time when Hugo wrote the novel, this dramatic marriage was an outrage to the class consciousness of Europe. It was a new song.

The new song in my mouth—the wedding song of the Sacred

Marriage—bears witness to the dawn of a new era of truth, liberty, and a deeper level of equality: true partnership. We must claim this reality for ourselves, in our own lives and homes, and we must seek to create the world of our new vision. The feminine principle bound on earth and in heaven cannot remain bound! Under the aegis of the Black Madonna, our chains and shackles are falling and the archetypal feminine as partner is emerging in consciousness—the Goddess rising. She is modeled on Magdalene, not Medusa! We need not turn our partners to stone, but we do need to be recognized at last as their long-lost "other half." But first, before we can claim our full legacy, we must find ways to heal the wounded feminine in our own hearts and souls.

As we have seen, direct evidence for the sacred union indigenous to Christianity is found embedded in the gematria of the New Testament texts themselves. The numbers coded in the New Testament, silent for centuries, are irrefutable and eloquent beyond words; the geometry they generate reflects the harmonious workings of the cosmos. For those initiated into the meaning of the sacred sums, for those who have eyes to see and ears to hear and are willing to receive the evidence, the meaning is as clear today as it was in the first century in Palestine and the surrounding Roman provinces.

Partnership—the freedom, equality, and fraternity of both sexes and all individuals was the original message of the Gospels, embedded in the gematria of the "grain of mustard seed!" For, the author of Genesis reminds us, "in God's own image God created them—male and female" (Gen. 1:27). And God says, "It is not good for man to be alone; I shall form for him a partner" (Gen. 2:18). Christ quotes from this same passage in Genesis in Matthew's Gospel, noting that "a man leaves his parents and clings to his wife, and the two become one flesh" and proclaiming that what God, therefore, has joined, no one should separate (19:6).

The legends of the Holy Grail insist that when the Grail is found, the desert wasteland ruled by the wounded Fisher-King will be healed. The Grail was said to be the chalice that once contained the blood of Christ, and knights in shining armor searched the length and breadth of Europe for the missing vessel. My research has led me to the inevitable conclusion that this lost vessel was not an artifact, but a woman: the lost Bride of Jesus who brought his child to France. In reclaiming this lost wife of Jesus we restore the lost Grail and the ancient mandala of the *hieros gamos* to Christianity.

From the dawn of the Christian era the sacred partners, Christ and Magdalene, were intended to provide an archetypal model for loving service and mutual devotion. Together these Beloveds incarnated the covenant of the eternal Bridegroom and the cosmic Bride—an image of the Divine as loving partners. This mandala, long heralded by mystics and now crystallizing in our own psyches, will help to heal our own intimate relationships and our personal woundedness, making us joyful, making us whole!

CHAPTER XII

THE SACRED REUNION

No longer will you be called forsaken and your lands "desolate," but you shall be called "beloved" and your lands, "espoused." (Isa. 62:4)

The close partnership of intuition and research related to the secret of the Grail has yielded a rich harvest in my life. The lost archetype of the Bride is inherent in the medieval mystery surrounding the Holy Grail, and the motifs of the lonely, crippled king and the wasteland that is his realm are imbued with multilayered symbolism that has been a source of enlightenment over the years of my quest.

When I speak now of reclaiming the lost Bride, I am at once thinking of restoring the historical wife of Jesus to her rightful place at his side and at the same time, on a deeper plane, thinking of how that will help to restore the "partnership paradigm"—the imaging of the Divine as both Bride and Bridegroom—in the holy inner sanctum of our collective psyche: "on earth as it is in heaven." We must value our own feelings and emotions, our own intuitions, our own experience, our own selves. We must honor our own journeys.

In the image of the dark Madonna, we encounter not just the human Mary who was the Jewish mother of Jesus, but rather the scorned and neglected "other face of God"—the entire feminine archetype that must be acknowledged before we can be whole. That dark, inscrutable lady is the parallel image—the "Sister-Bride"—of the lord of light and splendor, power and might, who comes riding on clouds of glory. With hideous scars mutilating her cheek, she represents the lowly, unsung, nearly nameless millions of God's people—the *anawim* in Hebrew—who carry the divine image just as surely and truly as do their revered saints, priests, and leaders. She embodies the communal, archetypal Bride in a larger and more profound sense than any one historical woman can—even the Blessed Virgin Mary or Mary Magdalene. So we must look at many facets of the sacred feminine in order to understand what we truly need to reclaim.

The celibate male image of God worshiped for nearly two thousand years of Western civilization is a distorted image that desperately pleads to be corrected. Our society mirrors what we worship. And we have been told over millennia that "he" is holy. The truth is that "she," too, is holy, in all her facets: maiden and mother, sister, daughter, lover, bride, and crone!

A correspondent once asked me if there were prophetic shadows of Mary Magdalene in the Hebrew Scriptures of the Old Testament, like the oft-cited prefigurations of Jesus. Examples include Isaac carrying the wood for his sacrifice up the mountain, as Christ carried the cross; or the suffering servant in Isaiah, led like a lamb to the slaughter; or Jonah tossed onto the beach after three days in the belly of the great fish.

My answer was, and still is, a resounding yes! There are numerous prophetic foreshadowings of Mary Magdalene, the Beloved, the Prostitute/Bride. One of the most obvious—already mentioned—is the Bride found in the Song of Songs: the Beloved, whom the Bridegroom calls "my Dove." This archetypal Bride is Wisdom incarnate—and the dove is her age-old totem. She is traditionally interpreted as a metaphor for the entire faith community.

Another shadow of the Magdalene is Hagar the Egyptian, the bondwoman who was banished from Abraham's household and forced to find her own way in the desert with her son Ishmael (Gen. 21). Hers was "the child of the flesh," while Sarah's son Isaac was "the child of the promise" (Gal. 4:23). And then there is the little naked and abused girl-child in Ezekiel 16, whom God found and pitied, clothed and nurtured. But she became wanton, casting her eyes at other lovers, the Old Testament symbol for the faithless community that runs after false gods.

And there is Gomer, the prostitute whom the prophet Hosea was told to marry. Even though she was unfaithful to him, he was told to take her back and forgive her repeated adultery as a sign of God's passionate and unconditional love for his people. Surely she was a shadow of "the Magdalene" as the symbol for the religious community, *ekklesia*, redeemed by the eternal Bridegroom.

There is the Hebrew place-name the "Magdal-eder"—"the watchtower/stronghold of Daughter Sion." Here the place-name represents the community of Israel sent into the fields and exiled, a condition prefiguring the refugee status of Magdalene who fled to France. Through "her," dominion would one day be restored (Mic. 4:8–10). One of the ancient epithets of Magdalene is "watchtower" or "stronghold"—the literal meaning of *magdala* in Hebrew.

In the book of Lamentations we find the distraught "Widow Sion," a personification of the desolate, vanquished people of Jerusalem. The faces of her descendants, the princes of the Davidic line, are now "blacker than soot" (Lam 4:8). They are unrecognized in the streets.

The Old Testament contains another prophetic shadow of the Bride of Jesus. The prototype of the Holy Grail is lodged in chapter 44 of Genesis. (I find it interesting that the Old Testament chapter containing the prototype of the "Grail" should arbitrarily bear the number 44—an echo of the number 444 which meant "flesh and blood" in the sacred canon of the ancients. This uniquely "feminine" number seems to foreshadow the archetypal earthen "chalice" and the womb!)

This passage in Genesis tells the story of the sons of Jacob, the patriarch of Israel. The sons of Leah, the elder wife, and of Jacob's concubines were jealous of Rachel's son Joseph and had sold him into slavery in Egypt. But he had survived to become the trusted advisor of the Pharaoh.

When his brothers came to buy food stored in Joseph's warehouses in Egypt, they did not recognize him. Before they left, Joseph had his servants hide his own silver drinking cup in the sack of his brother Benjamin. It was Joseph's intent to test his brothers by accusing them of stealing the cup and framing their youngest brother, Benjamin, their father's favorite son. When the silver cup was found by Joseph's servants, it became the instrument of the healing and reconciliation among the twelve sons of Jacob.

Because he was so well versed in the history and sacred texts of his people, I feel sure that Rabbi Jesus knew and loved this story of Joseph and his brothers found in the Book of Genesis. He himself was from the royal line of Judah, one of the two remaining tribes that had not become lost in the first destruction of Jerusalem and the subsequent exile of its people from their land. The other tribe still extant was that of Benjamin, the descendants of Joseph's precious little brother. Rachel, the favorite wife, had died giving birth to Benjamin. She had been buried close to the hillock called Magdal-eder near Bethlehem and was still beloved and esteemed in the heart of every Jew.

When it came time to choose his wife, Jesus must have somehow sensed that the vessel of his delight would be found "in the sack of Benjamin." The family of Lazarus was wealthy, and Mary was probably heiress to Benjaminite lands near Jerusalem. The marriage of Jesus and this Mary would have united the destinies of the two tribes—Judah and Benjamin—at a crucial moment in the history of Israel. This, I cheerfully admit, is a favorite romantic speculation of mine, submitted in light of the dictionary meaning of "speculation": "to see from a distance, as from a watchtower!" Why not? *Magdala* means "watchtower"!

Because Joseph's silver drinking cup had been hidden in Benjamin's sack of grain at a crucial moment, ultimately saving Israel from famine, it seems beautifully prophetic. The silver chalice hidden in the sack of Benjamin is the prototype of the Holy Grail. When it is finally recognized, it may well be an instrument for reconciliation among the nations.

We are not talking now about a legendary artifact, said to be the silver chalice from which Jesus drank at the Last Supper. We are referring to "a vessel of clay," the Magdalene, the Bride of Jesus. When this "other Mary," neglected for two thousand years, is acknowledged in her rightful place as the flesh-and-blood (444!) wife of Jesus, perhaps the schism between Judaism, Christianity, and Islam can be healed at last! Then all the tribes of the estranged human family can finally be reconciled, as each human heart begins to heal its own painful split and becomes integrated.

The words of another song, a country hit tune, return often to haunt me: "When the sun always shines, there's a desert below." The wasteland is a poignant theme in Western European literature—the wasteland that is healed when the Grail is found. The same waste-land is healed in fairy tales when the playboy prince finally finds his true counterpart and everyone in their kingdom lives happily ever after. It is an echo of the promised nuptials of the Lamb in the Apocalypse: water flows from the throne of God healing the nations (Rev. 22). It is the theme of well-loved films like *The Secret Garden* and *Enchanted April*, where the wounded masculine and feminine find healing in one another.

Another popular tale comes to mind, the adventures of little Bastian in *The Neverending Story*, who stepped into the pages of the book he was reading and was tasked to find the "Empress" and give her a new name. (*Has Pope John Paul II seen this film about little Bastian?* I've wondered. *Perhaps he should!*) Throughout the story, we hope for Bastian's success, picturing the Empress in full regalia, an imposing middle-aged matriarch like the Queen of England. But no. Finally at the end of the movie Bastian is face-to-face with the Empress, and SURPRISE! She is a child his own age, his mirror image, his counterpart—a playmate and a friend. He names her Moon-Child. How fitting! How perfectly, appropriately *feminine*!

The Sacred Marriage of the polarities is a mandala waiting to be understood as the underlying sacred principle of the universe, the lost blueprint that radiates peace and harmony, healing the wasted land. The intimate union of male and female is the source of all life on our planet, the model for life as we know it—there is no other!

This is the blueprint Mary Beben had written about in her journal in 1973 when Jan showed her the broken statue of Jesus with the lost piece of the foundation. She had then understood that a new blue-print was trying to be manifested in human consciousness, but that the current model had first to be destroyed. The ✡ is the blueprint for wholeness that is manifested in the psyche of the human person. As a model for the sacred "earthen vessel"—each human individ-ual—the Temple in Jerusalem with its outer and inner courts leading to the "Holy of Holies" was designed, according to Jewish mystics, to contain the presence of Yahweh and his holy consort, the Shekinah, dwelling together in intimate union in their "bridal chamber"[1]—the human psyche/heart.

I believe that the cracks in the foundation of Christianity are so profound and so dangerous that the whole edifice is now in danger of crumbling into ruins. Naming the Virgin Mary as Co-Redemptrix with Christ will reinforce one ancient mandala for wholeness: the mother/son mandala of the ancient world represented divinity as a union of opposites—male and female, young and old, big and small.

But this familiar model will not heal the wounds caused by the denial of the full humanity of Jesus and the human bride he loved. Instead, this proclamation of "Co-Redemptrix," if taken too literally, as dogmas tend to be, will perpetuate the exclusive "Virgin Mother/Celibate Son" orientation of Christianity that has yet to acknowledge the partnership role of the Bride, the other Mary of the Gospel story.

One chilly Sunday in mid-January 1992 I walked to mass at the chapel across the frost-covered parade field in front of our quarters at Fort Lewis. The publication of my research of the marriage of Jesus and Mary Magdalene was imminent. I had just that week signed a contract for *The Woman with the Alabaster Jar* and I was anxious. Although my pastor and chaplain friends were supportive of my work, my own father had recoiled from the idea of a married Jesus. A few friends and mentors had also expressed shock at my frank discus-sion of the mountain of circumstantial evidence that supports the marriage of Jesus.

Many people just do not want anyone to tamper with traditions concerning Christ. Some are hostile to the idea, even though they have never personally examined the issue at all! They just assume that Jesus was never married, since that is the party line of established Christianity. I was feeling apprehensive about the criticism and rejection I would surely face from many quarters, perhaps even from some of my friends, and certainly from clergy in the establishment. I had cold feet, but not from the frost on the grass. On that morning, I prayed earnestly for peace and solace.

Mass began with the usual opening prayers. The lector went to the podium, opened the red, leather-bound Bible, and began to read the prescribed passage from the Hebrew Scriptures, taken on this Sunday from the Book of Isaiah 62:1–4:

> For Sion's sake I will not be silent until her vindication
> shines forth   like the dawn. . . . No longer shall you be
> called "forsaken" and your lands "abandoned," but you shall
> be called "beloved" and your lands "espoused."

I began to cry softly, feeling the blessing of the verses like rain falling on my parched soul. I had come a long way on my journey, and I now felt reassured that I had not traveled alone.

In light of the traditions of Judaism and the concrete evidence encoded by gematria in the Gospels themselves, I am certain that Jesus was married and that the woman called Magdalene was his partner, his Beloved, and his wife. Incredible synchronicities along my path have confirmed this truth. Many friends who accompanied me on my journey have gradually affirmed the "good news" of this discovery, and many people have contacted me over the years since my first book was published to thank me for having had the courage to proclaim the return of the Bride. I sometimes smile, remembering the day in Nashville when I tried to give the Grail back to Jesus and ended up having dinner with French visitors, hearing the lore and legends surrounding Magdalene in Provence and the notes of the waiter's silver trumpet.

Since that time, my research has continued to center around the "sacred reunion," bringing to light many works of art and literature that corroborate my earlier work. Without doubt, Magdalene was the most prominent of the women in the Gospels, and devotion to her was strong in Western Europe until it was suppressed in the thirteenth century. Her honored status was gradually eroded, while epithets that once expressed her exalted position were transferred to the Virgin Mary. The only remnant of her former glory left to Magdalene was the unique spelling of her epithet—and the eloquent stone arches of the Gothic cathedrals formed in her image, the (), the 153.

Now at last we understand the persistent rumor that the masons of Europe built the tenets of their faith—the true Christian faith—into the stones of the Gothic cathedrals. The sacred stones of the vaulting arches in Europe's medieval churches themselves cry out to all who enter that they honor the Goddess, the eternal feminine. This includes, above all, the Magdalene, for the prevailing shape in Gothic architecture is the Vesica Piscis, and the underlying architectural principle in these magnificent churches is the intricate balancing of the opposite energies—the *hieros gamos*.

It is precisely this principle of balance that was understood by the Greek philosophers and alchemists and preached again in the twentieth century by Carl Jung and his disciples. This integration of male and female is fundamental to our healing—of ourselves, our families, our societies, our planet.

We are poised at the brink of the New Millennium, a time of unparalleled danger, and unparalleled hope! Conscious of the deep wounds we have suffered, we must concentrate our energies on healing our brokenness. I am still in the crucible of transformation. But I now know that no external power is going to save me. I am conscious of my own inner authority to envision a new path and of my responsibility to band with others of like vision to create the "new wineskins" needed to contain our hopes for a saner and healthier future on Earth.

This is the same process that the architects of Christianity embraced at the turn of their age. Like them, we will need commitment and courage to persevere amid the chaotic changes occurring in our societies.

The journey is never finished, the road is not always well marked, but the darkness and the light are playmates, the right and left hands are partners! Like courageous gypsies, those eternal pilgrims, we must travel light and sing and dance along the way, both creating and celebrating each moment.

At some point in my journey, I understood that my original goal had evolved into a much larger purpose. I now realize that I am charged not only with restoring the Bride to Christianity—the Goddess in the Gospels—but also with restoring the partnership paradigm that was the cornerstone of ancient civilizations and the archetypal blueprint not only for the Temple of Solomon, but for the human psyche as well. My current work includes winning friends for this "partnership paradigm" at the threshold of the new millennium.

An enlightened Church of the future will surely teach that each earthen vessel, male or female, is equally designed to be a sacred container for the Holy Spirit. This "Grail" spirituality has been neglected except for its brief flowering in the twelfth and thirteenth centuries. The doctrine of the sacred partnership of humanity *and* divinity in each human individual will be the fundamental tenet of a "Church of the Holy Spirit." Together the human family embodies the new entity, the Divine Child "Emmanuel," for Godde is with us. This will be the fundamental teaching of the new, enlightened community, the Church I now envision, the Church of the age to come.

Its faithful will be "water carriers"—tasked with bringing the waters of spirit and truth to heal the wasteland.

$$\Lambda$$
V

Ave Millennium—99

FUNDAMENTALS OF GREEK GEMATRIA[1]

The ancient system of gematria is based on the fact that there are no separate characters for numbers in classical Greek. Each letter was used as a number, and each number value carried symbolic meaning. Each Greek word written on a page could also be understood as a number, and the values of the digits could easily be added. Each of the twenty-four alphabet letters of the Greek alphabet was assigned a numerical value in a three-tiered sequence, and the sum of a word or phrase was easily calculated by adding together the values of all its individual alphabet letters.

Following is a list of the numerical values of letters in the Greek alphabet[2]:

A,α	B,β	Γ,γ	Δ,δ	E,ε	Z,ζ	H,η	Θ,θ
1	2	3	4	5	7	8	9

I,ι	K,κ	Λ,λ	M,μ	N,ν	Ξ,ξ	O,o	Π,π
10	20	30	40	50	60	70	80

P,ρ	Σ,σ,s	T,τ	Y,υ	Φ,φ	X,χ	Ψ,ψ	Ω,ω
100	200	300	400	500	600	700	800

When the values of the letters in a carefully contrived word or phrase were added together, the sum had a specific and sacred cosmic meaning, based on the symbolic numbers of their cosmology, universal numbers in use since the time of Plato and before.[3]

The fundamental number associated with the eternal feminine principle in the ancient canon of sacred geometry was 1080, and the same number is the value of the Greek letters in "the Holy Spirit" (*to agion pneuma*) and also "fountain of wisdom" (*phgh sophias*). The significance of the number 1080 was based originally on the calculation of the radius of the moon, and the feminine principle throughout the ancient Middle East was understood to be "lunar," the "Sister-Bride" who mirrored the light of the masculine sun.

The gematria for "dove" (περιστερα) is 801, an anagram for 1080, so the dove was chosen very early in history as an appropriate symbol for the Goddess. This same "totem" bird was later adopted by Christians to represent the Holy Spirit, whose sacred number is also 1080. So by gematria, the Holy Spirit is linked explicitly to the lunar or feminine principle and to the dove.

The revealing numbers continue to enlighten and delight the initiated who have "eyes to see and ears to hear." For example, the value of the letter *alpha* (A) was 1 in Greek, and the *omega* (Ω) was 800, making the dove the perfect symbol for the Spirit of the Living God—the "Alpha" and the "Omega": 801. The creative "Word of God" consisted of the entire cosmos, the sum of all reality and all possibilities, and therefore the total of every conceivable combination of alphabet letters: the "Alpha and the Omega."

In this phrase often used to describe the Creator, the sum of the actual digits—8 and 1—was 9, a number that meant "completion," and "the culmination of prophecy." The number 999, the "epitome" or "fullness" of 9 was a synonym for "judgment day," and Christian prayers, often ended with 99, the gematria for the word *amen* (amen): "So be it," or "Let it come to pass!"

The sophisticated and widespread practice of gematria by the authors of the New Testament permitted the sums of words to be cross-pollinated in this way to elucidate the philosophical principles in their sacred texts. It raised their writing to a higher plane, like setting its lines to music.

THE *Hieros Gamos* AND THE GRAIN OF MUSTARD SEED

K nowledge of New Testament gematria reveals that the *hieros gamos* was one of the original teachings of Christianity attributed directly to Jesus but obscured in later Church tradition. The number 666, the number of the beast in the Apocalypse, is related to the "magic square of the sun" and universally equated with the masculine/solar principle—the oriental "yang"—while the "yin" number 1080 is associated with the eternal feminine.[1]

Not accidentally, the Hebrew Scriptures record a yearly weight in gold paid in tribute to King Solomon was "666 golden talents" (2 Chr. 9:13). This phrase sums up the yang principle of tribute to the king. But the number is not evil in itself, nor is the cosmic principle it represents. Like yang, it represents "solar orientation": law, order, justice, righteousness, reason, victory—"banners waving in the sun." Yet we are all becoming aware that when the sun shines too intensely for too long the earth below becomes a desert, parched and desolate—the wasteland of legend. It suffers burnout.

In order to be safe, the solar principle must be "wedded" to its natural opposite, the feminine energy, the yin. Yoked together—only together!—they generate peace and harmony and well-being. Like positive and negative electric charges, they are dangerous until they are harnessed in union. The feminine, without the offsetting male principle, represents chaos, flood waters, and "the bottomless pit"— the "abyss." The qualities associated with the feminine principle— darkness, silence, intuition, gentleness, rain, and the "shady side of the mountain"—help to balance the positively charged "solar" qualities of the masculine.

The operative attribute of 666 is unadulterated power. The 666 in extreme isolation becomes the *beast*; crocodiles, the totem of Egypt's pharaohs, are the extreme example. What do they have for dinner? Anything they want! Like despotic rulers, they epitomize the solar 666 without its feminine counterbalance, the lunar 1080. But the feminine principle alone—the chaos and havoc wrought by flood—is just as dangerous as the masculine principle without its partner. Balance is harmony.

In classical philosophy both lunar and Earth principles were considered receptive or "feminine," while the solar principle was understood to be the active, "positive" energy of the masculine. The sum of the numbers 666 and 1080—representing the *hieros gamos* union of the two opposite principles—is 1746. Plato called this number "the Same and the Other" and "fusion."[2]

Jesus is quoted: "The kingdom of God is like a grain of mustard seed," Κοκκος σιναπεως (*kokkos sinapeōs*). The three synoptic Gospels of Mark, Matthew, and Luke contain this metaphor of the grain of mustard seed, as does the Gnostic Gospel of Thomas found among the Nag Hammadi scrolls. In the Greek system of gematria, the sum of the phrase "a grain of mustard seed" is 1746, "fusion." It is the sacred seed of the cosmos, representing the union of the opposite energies, positive and negative, male and female: the "Sacred Marriage." Hidden in the gematria of the "grain of mustard seed" for two thousand years is found the true doctrine of the reign of God: The formula for the promised kingdom of heaven on earth is the harmonious balance of the masculine and feminine represented by the ✡ .

APPENDIX 3

THE HOLY NAME OF MARY AND THE VESICA PISCIS

By gematria the Greek name Maria is 152. By the conventions of the system, one unit, called a *colel* in Hebrew, may be added or subtracted from a sum without changing its symbolic significance. When the *colel* of +1 allowed by the system is added, the gematria of *Maria* becomes 153, one of the most significant of all numbers in the geometry of the ancient Greeks. In their sacred canon of number, 153 was universally recognized by those educated in mathematics as the number designating the geometric shape known as "the measure of the fish"—the Vesica Piscis in Latin.[1] This number was commonly used as an abbreviation of the fraction 265/153, the ratio used to represent the square root of three (just as 22/7 was used for the ratio of a circle's circumference to its diameter—"pi" or π). A Vesica Piscis () with a horizontal axis of 1 has a vertical axis of 265/153. Among Greek mathematicians, this shape was called simply the "153."

A Vesica Piscis is formed when two circles intersect, and the sacred () shape was extremely important in ancient geometry, for it represented the "womb" or "matrix" of all other geometric derivations. This highly significant symbol is a "seed" shape, often called the "almond" or "mandorla" (Italian) in art, and referred to as the "vulva," or "gateway," emphasizing its distinctly feminine connotations. These include the fertility and regeneration of which the feminine is the threshold. It was the "matrix" (the mother!) from which all other geometric figures were derived. It was also known in the ancient world as "the Holy of Holies"—the "inner sanctum." The Vesica Piscis is said to symbolize life and the "materialization of the Spirit,"[2] an important function reserved to the feminine! The shape represented, quite literally, the eternal creation of the "Earth-Grail," the "gateway" or source of all life. Her essence is "mother of all that lives."

All the New Testament women named Maria (Mary) are associated with this important feminine principle by virtue of the gematria of their shared name Maria, 152. But the epithet of one Mary, the Magdalene, η Μαγδαληνη, bears the exact sum 153. Can it be an accident that the gematria for "the Magdalene" is the universally recognized number of the Vesica Piscis from the ancient canon of sacred geometry? Hardly! Attributes of the Vesica are given to anyone bearing the name Mary, but it is the Magdalene alone—of all her sex!—whose epithet bears the exact number 153 associated with the Vesica Piscis and with the archetypal feminine. She was thus specifically designated as the Goddess in the Gospels, a profound truth hidden for two millennia in the encoded gematria of her name!

A BEACON TO GOD'S REALM

In the middle of all their quarrels
God will strike a giant bell
For a Slavonic Pope, as He empties the Throne.
This one will not shrink from critics like the others,
Fearless as Christ, he will face all courageously.
His world—just a mire!

His countenance a radiating lamp for service,
And men will follow this beacon to God's realm.
To his prayers, not only his people, but others will listen;
This charism, a miracle!

He is already approaching, the dispenser of a new global force;
His words will cause a pause and reflection
As a stream of divine light floods all hearts.
His understanding and wisdom are of the Spirit,
The energy needed to raise up the Lord's world.

And so comes the Slavonic Pope, all people's brother,
Who will bring vitality and rebirth to all.
A choir of angels adorns with graces the Throne,
For he will teach Love and not, as other leaders, reaching for arms.

His sacramental strength will emanate to the world;

The Dove will guide his thoughts and actions
To bring this good news of the Spirit's presence.
Heaven will open in complete accord
Because he stands and unites the world to the Throne.

Humanity will embrace in brotherhood at his call
And the Spirit will reach out to the farthest lands.
A solemn dignity, as of the Spirit, will be visible.
Such a one you will see soon—a shadow and then his face.

He will purge all decay, pretense, revolt and sham;
He will dispel all ills and ventilate the interiors of churches
And even brighten and renew the entries.
He will bring health, charity, truth and salvation to earth;
God will shine as the dawn on all creation!

(Julius Slowacki, 1848. Translated by Bertha Wirtz.)

This poem, freely circulated in 1978 soon after Pope John Paul II was elected, was written more than a hundred years before the event. The prophetic fervor of the poem, the emotional hyperbole, and the ecstatic enthusiasm of the Polish author is understandable when we consider that there had never been a Polish or Slavic pope. The language is typical of pieces extolling the "miracle" of a "savior-hero," and at the time it was written, it reflected the chaos of the revolutions that were sweeping the capitals of Europe. It was a time of turbulence, and the apocalyptic hope of the masses for a world leader or "savior" who would herald peace and justice is characteristic. Similar poems were written about Napoleon. We can easily understand the ardent desire of the Polish poet for a charismatic Slavic pope and notice that this poem fits the genre of apocalyptic poetry.

Incredibly, the poem turns out to have been prophetic against all odds. All but a tiny handful of Roman Catholic popes have been Italians, and those few were a medieval Dutchman, an Englishman, and several Frenchmen (during the "Babylonian Captivity" of the fourteenth century when a papal court rivaling that in Rome was established in Avignon by the French king). The election of a Polish pope to the throne of Peter in 1978 was truly astonishing, an event that inspired and encouraged his countrymen in their struggle to face down and depose an oppressive Communist "puppet" regime.

The new "global force" mentioned in the poem can now be seen to be the liberation of the "feminine," a struggle encouraged and whetted by interest in the scarred face of Our Lady of Czestochowa since 1978 as well as in other Black Madonna images of Western Europe and those of goddesses from the ancient world. The "Dove" is, of course, a reference to the Holy Spirit, but significantly, also the traditional totem of the Triple Goddess of the ancients. And the "shadow" that preceded the "face" of the charismatic pope was Albino Luciano (whose name means "white light"): John Paul I, the diminutive, humble pope of the thirty-three-day pontificate, from August 26 to September 28, 1978. The Polish pope honored Luciano by choosing his papal name and thereby extended his presence and influence into the dawn of a new millennium: "the shadow, then the face."

Clearly the hyperbole of some of the lines has yet to be realized. Purging the world of all pretense and sham seems to lie beyond the jurisdiction of any human leader. This poem's relevance lies not in the fact that all of its lines have proven to be prophetic, but rather in the fact that any of them have! Slowacki's poem reflects a longing of the heart, not necessarily a vision of the eye.

N O T E S

PREFACE

1. See appendix 1 for an explanation of the Greek system of *gematria* and numerical equivalents for each letter of the Greek alphabet.

2. Michael Drosnin, *The Bible Code* (New York: Simon and Schuster, 1997).

3. See Elaine Pagels, *The Gnostic Gospels* (New York: Vintage Books, 1981) for a readable discussion of the Nag Hammadi texts and their strong traditions of the sacred feminine, especially that embodied in Mary Magdalene.

4. Susan Haskins, *Mary Magdalene, Myth and Metaphor* (New York: Harcourt Brace & Company, 1993), 40.

CHAPTER I

1. Harold Bayley, *The Lost Language of Symbolism* (Totowa, New Jersey: Rowman and Littlefield, 1974) vol. 1, 170-171. First published Great Britain: Williams and Norgate, 1912.

2. Margaret Starbird, *The Woman with the Alabaster Jar* (Santa Fe, NM: Bear & Company, 1993), 71-73.

3. This quote is taken from the *Paschalis Carminis* by Caelius Sedulius, the source of the title of a recent book on the cult of the Virgin Mary, *Alone of All Her Sex* by Marina Warner (New York: Alfred A. Knopf, Inc., 1983.) First published London: George Weidenfeld & Nicolson, Ltd., 1976. The entire phrase translated from the Latin reads: "Alone of all her sex, she pleased Christ."

CHAPTER II

1. Starbird, 62-63.

2. Ibid., for detailed discussion of the medieval heresy and Church of the Holy Grail, especially chapters 4 and 5. For discussion of the legends of the *sangraal* and the royal bloodline of Israel, see chapter 3.

3. James Robinson, ed. "The Gospel of Philip" in *The Nag Hammadi Library: In English* (San Francisco: Harper & Row, 1981), 136. First published Leiden, The Netherlands: E.J. Brill, 1978.

4. See William Phipps, *Was Jesus Married?* (New York: Harper & Row, 1970) and *The Sexuality of Jesus* (New York: Harper & Row, 1973) for detailed, scholarly, Scripture-based discussion of the marriage of Jesus in the context of Jewish practice of the first century.

5. See Marjorie M. Malvern, *Venus in Sackcloth* (Edwardsville, IL: University of Southern Illinois Press, 1975) for discussion of the anointing and the reunion of Jesus and Mary Magdalene in medieval miracle plays.

6. See Starbird, 35-47, for discussion of ancient myths of the sacrificed King and Jewish prophecy concerning the bloodline of David the King.

7. See Haskins, 80, for discussion of early Church tradition of Mary Magdalene as the "New Eve."

8. Ibid., 40. Haskins's book contains discussion of the Magdalene as representative of the Sophia in the works of early Christian exegetes of the New Testament.

9. Robinson, ed. "The Thunder Perfect Mind" in *The Nag Hammadi Library*, op. cit., 271.

10. For detailed discussion of the early associations of the zodiac with Jesus and the Christian way, see John Michell, *The Dimensions of Paradise: The Proportions and Symbolic Numbers of Ancient Cosmology* (San Francisco: Harper & Row, 1990), 195-198. First published London: Thames and Hudson Ltd., 1988. See also *The City of Revelation* (London: Garnstone Press, 1971), 91. Jesus as the Lord of the Age of Pisces is also discussed at some length by Carl G. Jung in *Aion* (Princeton, NJ: The Princeton University Press, 1968).

11. See Ute Ranke-Heinemann, *Eunuchs for the Kingdom of Heaven: Women, Sexuality and the Catholic Church*, trans. Peter Heinegg (New York: Doubleday, 1990) for exhaustive research and readable discussion of the historical emphasis on virginity and celibacy in the Roman Catholic Church. First published as *Eunuchen für das Himmelreich* (Munich: Knaur, 1989).

CHAPTER III

1. Haskins, 91.

2. Starbird, 27-29. The identification of Mary of Bethany with Mary Magdalene in the West is ancient. Both women are identified as the woman who anointed Christ with nard, and therefore with the Bride from the Song of Songs, whose nard wafted around her Bridegroom seated at the banquet.

3. William Phipps, *Was Jesus Married?* A majority of the critical scholars who participated in the Jesus Seminar did not believe that Jesus was celibate and thought that he had a special relationship with "Mary of Magdala." See their findings summarized in: Robert W. Funk et al, eds., *The Five Gospels* (New York: MacMillan Publishing Co., 1993), 220-221.

CHAPTER IV

1. The prophecies received by various members of the Emmanuel community are recorded in their private journals dating from 1973. These are unpublished, but

verifiable documents of this spiritual community of intercessors for the Roman Catholic Church and priesthood, formed on February 20, 1975, and consecrated on May 29, 1979.

2. Julius Slowacki, "A Beacon to God's Realm," trans. Bertha Wirtz, appears in appendix 4. I have never seen this poem printed in English but was sent a typewritten copy in 1979 by a friend. This translation was circulated freely among interested parties during the months following Karol Wotyla's election as Pope John Paul II in September 1978.

3. Ean Begg, *The Cult of the Black Virgin* (New York: Penguin Books, 1985), 249.

CHAPTER V

1. See John Michell, *The Dimensions of Paradise*, 51-53, for a complete discussion of the meanings of the digits 1 through 9 in the ancient canon.

2. See appendix 2 for a detailed discussion of the "kingdom of heaven" and the *gematria* of its metaphor, the "grain of mustard seed."

3. Tons Brunés, *The Secrets of Ancient Geometry—and Its Use*, trans. Charles M. Napier (Copenhagen: Rhodos, 1967), 248-249.

4. Haskins, 96. "Homily XXXIII" of Pope Gregory the Great is quoted, probably delivered in A.D. 591 at the Basilica of Saint Clement in Rome.

CHAPTER VI

1. Michael Baigent, Richard Leigh, and Henry Lincoln, *Holy Blood, Holy Grail* (New York: Little, Brown & Co., 1983). First published as *The Holy Blood and the Holy Grail* (London: Jonathan Cape, Ltd., 1982).

2. David Yallop, *In God's Name* (New York: Bantam Books, 1984).

3. Marie-Louise von Franz, *Alchemy* (Toronto: Inner City Books, 1980), 180-181.

4. Harold Bayley, *The Lost Language of Symbolism*.

5. See Starbird, 89-101, for discussion and drawings of Albigensian watermarks related to the Grail heresy.

6. Ibid., 76.

CHAPTER VII

1. Richard Cavendish, *The Tarot* (New York: Crescent Books, 1975).

2. For my interpretation of the tarot cards and color reproductions of the sixteen extant trumps of the Charles VI see Starbird, 104-106 and color plates 1-16.

3. See Baigent, Leigh, and Lincoln, 106-108, for discussion of the Order of the Knights of the Temple and their connection with the medieval Grail family.

4. Bayley, vol. 1, p. 26.

CHAPTER VIII

1. See appendix 2 for the *gematria* of the solar and lunar principles and their symbolic meanings in the ancient canon of sacred geometry, unchanged since the time of Plato (4th century B.C.).

CHAPTER IX

1. Emma Jung suggests that Grail stories circulated in the oral traditions of Western Europe as early as the eighth or ninth century, a date synchronous with early versions of *Cinderella*. See Emma Jung and Marie-Louise von Franz, *The Grail Legend*, trans. Andrea Dykes (London: Hodder and Stoughton, 1971). First published as *Graalslegende in psychologischer Sicht*.

2. One important example of this grouping of statues exists in the crypt of the cathedral at Metz, a town in Lorraine, France. This grouping is reputed to have been common in Templar chapels, probably because it stresses the presence of the family, but not the apostles, at the deposition and entombment. Those present include Martha and the three Marys: the Magdalene, the Virgin, and Mary Salome; Joseph of Arimathea, Nicodemus, and Lazarus (often identified with the apostle John).

3. An example of this grouping of statues is found in the Musée de l'Oeuvre Notre-Dame in Strasbourg, France.

4. Haskins, 40.

5. Robinson, ed., "The Gospel of Mary" in *The Nag Hammadi Library*, op. cit., 473.

CHAPTER X

1. See Michell, *The Dimensions of Paradise*, 193-195, for detailed discussion of the first-century Christian associations with the astrological signs.

2. See appendix 2 for discussion of the solar number 666 in the ancient canon of sacred geometry.

3. See appendix 1 for discussion of the *gematria* of *peristera*, "dove," and its implications.

4. F. Edward Hulme, *Symbolism in Christian Art* (London: Swan, Sonnenschein & Co., 1891), 203.

5. *The Dimensions of Paradise* by John Michell contains *gematria* values for many names, epithets, and phrases found in the canonical New Testament. A second valuable resource for New Testament *gematria* is David Fideler's *Jesus Christ, Sun of God: Ancient Cosmology and Early Christian Symbolism* (Wheaton, IL: Quest Books, 1993). See also *Theomatics: God's Best Kept Secret Revealed* by Jerry Lucas

and Del Washburn (New York: Stein & Day, 1977) for further detailed analysis of New Testament phrases by *gematria*. See appendix 1 for the *gematria* value of each letter of the Greek alphabet.

6. See appendix 2 for discussion of meaning of 666, the solar "number of the beast" gleaned from discussion of the canon of sacred geometry in Michell, *The Dimensions of Paradise*, 178-190.

7. Michell, *The Dimensions of Paradise*, 10.

CHAPTER XI

1. See appendix 1 for values of Greek letters for Maria and η Μαγδαληνη.

2. See Michell, *The Dimensions of Paradise*, 174-178, and Fideler, 291-301, for detailed interpretation of the geometry story problem in John 21, "the fishes" and "the net." The Greek words for both "fishes" and "the net" have *gematria* of 1224.

3. Fideler, 211 and 307. Fideler discusses the Vesica Piscis at length and the use of 153 to represent the figure. See also Michell, *The Dimensions of Paradise*, 71-73 and 79 for discussion of the "generative properties" of the Vesica Piscis, the "matrix" of sacred geometry. In addition, see Jonathan Hale, *The Old Way of Seeing* (Boston: Houghton Mifflin, 1994), 76. Pages 76-85 of this volume contain eloquent discussion of the Vesica Piscis in architecture and its symbolism.

4. Baigent, Leigh, and Lincoln, especially chapters 5-8.

5. See appendix 2 for an explanation of the *hieros gamous* inherent in the *gematria* of the "grain of mustard seed."

CHAPTER XII

1. Raphael Patai, *The Hebrew Goddess* (Hoboken, NJ: KTAV Publishing House, 1967), 178.

APPENDIX 1

1. John Michell's works, contain detailed scholarly discussion of the *gematria* found in the New Testament texts. See *The Dimensions of Paradise*, 178-84, for discussion of the lunar number 1080. Also 56-64: "Gematria: the names and numbers of God," and 170-198: "Symbolic Number." See 51-53 for meanings of the numbers 1 through 9.

2. Ibid., 59. The Greek letters used for the numbers 6, (*digamma*), 90 (*koppa*), and 900 (*sampi*) are no longer in use. See 59-60 for further explanation. Also, Fideler, 27.

3. Michell, *The Dimensions of Paradise*, 9.

APPENDIX 2

1. Michell explains the properties of the solar number 666 and the lunar 1080 in *The Dimensions of Paradise*, 178-190, and in *The City of Revelation*, 137-155, his two profound works dealing with the *gematria* of the New Testament.

2. Michell, *The City of Revelation*, 91.

APPENDIX 3

1. Fideler, 211 and 307. Fideler discusses the Vesica Piscis at length and the use of 153 to represent the figure. See also Michell, *The Dimensions of Paradise*, 71-73 and 79, for discussion of the "generative properties" of the Vesica Piscis, the "*matrix*" of sacred geometry.

2. Jonathan Hale, 76. See 76-85 for discussion of the Vesica Piscis in architecture.

APPENDIX 4

1. Please see chapter 4 of the notes, note 2. I am not aware of any translation of this poem published in English.

S E L E C T E D
B I B L I O G R A P H Y

Baigent, Michael, Richard Leigh, and Henry Lincoln. *The Holy Blood and the Holy Grail*. London: Jonathan Cape, Ltd., 1982. Reprint, *Holy Blood, Holy Grail*. New York: Dell Publishing Co., 1983.

Bayley, Harold. *The Lost Language of Symbolism*. Totowa, NJ: Rowman & Littlefield, 1974. First published Great Britain: Williams & Norgate, 1912.

Begg, Ean. *The Cult of the Black Virgin*. New York, Penguin Books, 1985.

Brandon, S. G. F. *Jesus and the Zealots*. New York: Charles Scribner's Sons, 1967.

Brown, Raymond E.. *The Community of the Beloved Disciple*. New York: Paulist Press, 1979.

———, ed. *The Jerome Biblical Commentary*. New Jersey: Prentice-Hall, 1968.

Brunés, Tons. *The Secrets of Ancient Geometry—and Its Use*. Translated by Charles M. Napier. Copenhagen: Rhodos, 1967.

Cartlidge, David R., and David L. Dungan, eds. *Documents for Study of the Gospels*. Philadelphia: Fortress Press, 1980.

Cavendish, Richard. *The Tarot*. New York: Crescent Books, 1975.

Charpentier, Louis. *The Mysteries of Chartres Cathedral*. Translated by Ronald Fraser and Janette Jackson. Northhamptonshire: Thorsons Publishers, Ltd., 1972.

Cruden, Alexander. *Cruden's Unabridged Concordance*. Grand Rapids, MI: Baker Book House, 1973.

Danielou, Jean. *The Dead Sea Scrolls and Primitive Christianity*. Translated by Salvator Attanasio. New York: New American Library, Mentor Omega Books, 1962.

Drosnin, Michael. *The Bible Code*. New York: Simon and Schuster, 1997.

Eisler, Riane. *The Chalice and the Blade*. San Francisco: Harper & Row, 1988.

Fideler, David. *Jesus Christ, Sun of God*. Wheaton, IL: Quest Books, 1993.

Funk, Robert W., et al, eds. *The Five Gospels*. New York: MacMillan Publishing Co., 1993.

Franz, Marie-Louise von. *Alchemy*. Toronto: Inner City Books, 1980.

Gettings, Fred. *The Secret Zodiac*. London: Routledge & Kegan Paul, 1987.

Hale, Jonathan. *The Old Way of Seeing*. Boston: Houghton Mifflin, 1994.

Halliday, W. R. *The Pagan Background of Early Christianity*. New York: Cooper Square Publishers, Inc., 1970.

Hanson, Paul D. *Visionaries and Their Apocalypses*. Philadelphia: Fortress Press, 1983.

Haskins, Susan. *Mary Magdalene, Myth and Metaphor*. New York, Harcourt Brace & Co., 1993.

Hulme, F. Edward. *Symbolism in Christian Art*. London: Swan, Sonnenschein & Co., 1891. Reprint, Detroit: Gale Research Co., 1969.

Inman, Thomas. *Ancient Pagan and Modern Christian Symbolism*. 1884. Reprint, Williamstown, MA: Corner House Publishers, 1978.

Jenkins, Ferrell. *The Old Testament in the Book of Revelation*. Grand Rapids, MI: Baker Book House, 1972.

Jung, Emma, and Marie-Louise von Franz. *The Grail Legend*. Translated by Andrea Dykes. London: Hodder and Stoughton, 1971. First published as *Graalslegende in psychologischer Sicht*.

Kelly, J. N. D. *Early Christian Creeds*. New York: David McKay Co., Inc., 1972.

Kramer, Samuel N. *The Sacred Marriage Rite*. Bloomington, IN: Indiana University Press, 1969.

Laws, Sophie. *In the Light of the Lamb*. Wilmington, DE: Glazier, Inc., 1988.

Lucas, Jerry, and Del Washburn. *Theomatics: God's Best Kept Secret Revealed*. New York: Stein & Day, 1977.

Malvern, Marjorie. *Venus in Sackcloth*. Edwardsville, IL: Southern Illinois University Press, 1975.

Michell, John. *The City of Revelation*. London: Garnstone Press, 1971.

————, *The Dimensions of Paradise: The Proportions and Symbolic Numbers of the Ancient Cosmology*. San Francisco: Harper & Row, 1990. First published London: Thames and Hudson, Ltd., 1988.

Pagels, Elaine. *The Gnostic Gospels*. New York: Vintage Books, 1981.

Patai, Raphael. *The Hebrew Goddess*. Hoboken, NJ: KTAV Publishing House, 1967.

Phipps, William. *Was Jesus Married?* New York: Harper & Row, 1970.

————, *The Sexuality of Jesus*. New York: Harper & Row, 1973.

Pope, Marvin H. *Song of Songs*. (Anchor Bible Series) Garden City: Doubleday & Co., Inc., 1983.

Qualls-Corbett, Nancy. *The Sacred Prostitute*. Toronto: Inner City Books, 1988.

Ranke-Heinemann, Uta. *Eunuchs for the Kingdom of Heaven: Women, Sexuality and the Catholic Church*. Translated by Peter Heinegg. New York: Doubleday, 1990.

First published as *Eunuchen für das Himmelreich*. Munich: Knaur, 1989.

Ringgren, Helmer. *Religions of the Ancient Near East*. Translated by John Sturdy. Philadelphia: Westminster Press, 1973.

Robinson, James M., ed. *The Nag Hammadi Library: In English*. New York: Harper & Row, 1981. First published Leiden, The Netherlands: E. J. Brill, 1978.

Silberer, Herbert. *Hidden Symbolism of Alchemy and the Occult Arts*. New York: Moffat, Yard & Co., 1917. Reprint, New York: Dover Publications, 1971.

Sparks, H. F. D., ed. *The Apocryphal Old Testament*. New York: Oxford University Press, 1984.

Starbird, Margaret. *The Woman with the Alabaster Jar: Mary Magdalene and the Holy Grail*. Santa Fe: Bear & Co., 1993.

Stone, Merlin. *When God Was a Woman*. New York: The Dial Press, 1976.

Vermes, G. *The Dead Sea Scrolls in English*. New York: Penguin Books, 1987.

Walker, Barbara. *The Woman's Dictionary of Symbols and Sacred Objects*. San Francisco: Harper & Row, 1988.

———, *The Woman's Encyclopedia of Myths and Secrets*. San Francisco: Harper & Row, 1983.

Warner, Marina. *Alone of All Her Sex*. New York: Alfred A. Knopf, 1983. First published London, George Weidenfeld & Nicolson, 1976.

Yallop, David. *In God's Name*. New York: Bantam Books, 1984.

BIBLES

Holy Bible: New International Version. New York: The American Bible Society, 1978.

Saint Joseph New Catholic Edition of the Holy Bible. New York: Catholic Book Publishing Co., 1963.

I N D E X

Abraham, 74, 120, 146

Adonis, 24, 132

Age of Aquarius, 134

Age of Aries, 130

Age of Pisces, 127-131, 133, 141

Age of Taurus, 130

Albigensian, 10, 82, 142

Alpha, the, and the Omega, 109, 156

anawim, 121, 146

Anfortas, 87

Apocalypse (of John), 123, 149, 157
(*see also* Revelation, Book of)

Apollo, 126

Arian, 125

Artemis, 9

Baal, 108

Babylon, 49, 60, 72, 107, 138

Baigent, Michael, 85

Bastian, 149

Bayley, Harold, 78, 82, 85

Beben, Mary, ix, 42, 46, 56, 58, 67,
107, 111, 133, 149

Benjamin, 148

Bible Code, The (Drosnin), xii

Black Madonna, xiii-xiv, 14, 31-33, 49-
50, 52, 111, 115, 143, 163 (*see also*
Czestochowa, Our Lady of)
feast of the, 16
shrine(s) of the, 5, 17

Black Rose, The (Costain), 33-34, 37

blade (the fire triangle), 129

Blessed Mother, 48, 118 (*see also* Virgin
Mary)

blueprint (for body of Christ), 42-43,
51, 60, 103, 150, 153
sacred, 59

Boaz, 86

Book of Acts, 17

Bride, 27, 37, 52, 63, 70, 76, 95, 115-
116, 121, 137, 139-140, 144, 151,
153
and Bridegroom, 22-23, 25
dark, 29, 31-32, 34, 35
lost, 28, 61, 62, 113, 122, 145
of Christ, 7, 38, 60, 147
Sister, 33

Bridegroom, 16, 22-26, 32, 36, 61, 64,
126-127, 144, 145, 147
crippled, 95
/King, 9, 24
prophecy, 60

Brother Lawrence, 72

Bull, the (Age of Taurus), 130

Cabala, 68, 70

Candlemas, 16

Canticle of Canticles (the Canticle) ,
31-32, 34-35, 76, 116 (*see also* Song
of Solomon, Song of Songs)

Cathar(s), 10, 29, 31, 87, 90

Challenger, 68, 70-71, 75, 77, 107

Charles VI tarot, 82, 83, 86

Chartres, 11, 38

Christology, 125

Church of Amor (Church of Love), 10, 85, 87, 121

Cinderella, 32, 101, 103, 105, 115

City of Revelation, The (Michell), 128

Clement of Alexandria, 127

Clermont-Ferrand, 11

Co-Redemptrix, xiv, 50, 52, 64, 133, 150

colel, 140, 159

conjunctio, 8, 36, 51

Constantine, 56

Costain, Thomas B., 33-34

Cybele, 9, 38

Cyrus, 48-51

Czestochowa, Our Lady of, xiv, 9, 32, 48, 50-52, 76, 163 (*see also* Black Madonna of)

Dates
9th of Av, 56-58, 61, 132
18 May (1980), 53
18 May (1996), 5
25 May (1980), 54, 63
29 May (1979), 76
22 July (1980), 56-58, 61

David (King), 17, 25, 26, 74, 84, 86-87, 95

Demeter, 26

Dionysus, 132

dove, 32, 90-91, 163, 124, 146, 156, 161, 163

Drosnin, Michael, xii

Dumuzi, 24

Ebionite, 125

eclipse, 8, 36, 51, 101

ekklesia, 7, 32, 140, 147

Emmanuel community, ix, 48, 54, 56, 58, 61, 63, 65-67, 69, 73, 76, 89, 111
charismatic, xii
history of, 41-47

Enchanted April, 149

Fishes (also fishes), 127-128, 131, 140-141

fleur-de-lis, 15, 85

Fortress Antonio, 90

Freemason(ry), 60, 77, 86

fusion, 158

Galatians, 74

gematria, 9-10, 27, 123, 132, 151, 156, 157-158
definition, xii-xiii
for fishes, 141
for Mary, 140, 159, 160
for Mary Magdalene, 139-140
in Michell, 128, 129
in number 8, 128
numerical values, 155
sacred number, 59

Genesis, 20, 147-148

Gnostic(s), xv, 17, 26, 35, 119-121, 158

Godde, 109, 114-115, 134, 153

Gomer (wife of Hosea), 147

Gospel of
John (*also* John's Gospel), 25, 35
Luke (*also* Matthew's Gospel), 35, 158
Mark (*also* Mark's Gospel), 127, 158
Matthew (*also* Matthew's Gospel), 143, 158

Gospel of Mary, 119

Gospel of Philip, 17, 119

Gospel of Thomas, 158

Grail, the, xi, 14, 78, 81, 84, 87, 91, 96, 114, 149, 151, 153 (see also Holy Grail)

eternal vessel, 52

heresy, 77-78, 85, 111, 113, 115, 142

in Templar chapel, 119

mystery of the, 25

grain of mustard seed, 59, 143, 158

Guadalupe, Our Lady of, 89

Hagar (mother of Ishmael), 146

Hagia Sophia, 7, 32

hexagram, 90 91

hieros gamous, xiii, 8, 24, 26, 38, 60, 135, 144, 152, 157-158

Hippolytus of Rome, 63, 116

Holy Blood, Holy Grail, 65, 67, 72, 77, 85, 142

Holy Grail, xv, 7, 13, 39, 77-79, 111-112, 115, 143, 145

and tarot, 82

as sacred container, 121

Church of the, 17, 78, 82

heresy of, 66, 88

legend of the, 28

prototype in Genesis, 147-148

Holy Sophia, 9, 26

Holy Wisdom, xii, 7, 26, 38

Horus, 9

Hugo, Victor, 142

Ichthys, 127, 131, 133, 141

Ihsous, 128, 131, 133, 140

In God's Name (Yallop), 66, 67-68

Inanna, 9, 38, 96

Inquisition, 10, 78, 84-86, 88

Isaac, 146

Ishmael, 146

Isis, 9, 16, 38

Isis/Horus, 10

Jacob, 147-148

Jasna Gora, 51

Jericho, 82

Jesus Seminar, 10

Job, 133

Jonah, 146

Joseph, 147-148

Joshua, 45

Judah, 86-87, 148

Jung, Carl, 75, 90, 152

King Louis XI, 85

Knights of the Temple of Solomon, The, 83 (see also Knights Templar, Templars)

Knights of the Temple, 87-88

Knights Templar, 86

koinonōs, xv

Kyrios, 126-128, 131, 133

Ladyhawke, 36, 101

Lamb (of God), 25, 127, 130, 149

Lamentations, 147

Langue d'oc, 121

Languedoc, 10, 29, 87

lapis exillis, 17

Lazarus, xiii, 13, 16-17, 34-35, 63, 113-114-115, 148

Les Misérables (Hugo), 141-142

Les Saintes-Maries-de-la-Mer, 11, 13, 15, 63, 113

Lion of Judah, 25

Logos, 129

Longinus, 90-91

Lost Language of Symbolism, The (Bayley), 78, 85

Lourdes, 11

Luciano, Albino, 46-47, 67, 163 (see also Pope John Paul I)

Magdal-eder, 147-148

Magdala, 15, 87, 147-148

Magdalene, (the), 24, 34, 61-62, 64, 140, 152, 160

Marseilles, 11

Martha, xiii, 16, 34, 63, 113

Mary of Bethany, 25, 34-35, 62-63, 113

matrix, 140, 159-160

Merovingian(s), 15, 17, 51, 85-86, 118

Messiah, 23, 25, 126

Metz, 118

Michelangelo, 108

Michell, John, 78, 128, 139

Michol (King David's wife), 74

Miriam, 33-34, 36-37

Mithraism, 130

Montsegur, 13, 87

Montserrat, 11

Mount Saint Helens, 53-57, 59, 61-64

Nag Hammadi, xv, 17, 26, 119, 121, 158

nard, 24, 35

National Aeronautics and Space Administration (NASA), 70-71

navettes, 16

Nebuchadnezzar, 56, 132

Neverending Story, The 149

New Eve, 26

New Light on the Renaissance (Bayley), 82

Nicene Creed, 125

Noli Me Tangere, 25

Notre Dame de la Confessione, 15, 17

number of the beast, 129, 157-158 (see also Numbers: "666")

Numbers
"7", 71, 76, 130-131
"8", 128, 131, 141, 156
"9", 57, 156
"99", 156
"153", 129, 140-141, 152, 159
"444", 147, 149
"666", 124, 129, 157-158
"800", 128
"801", 156
"888", 128, 131, 139-140
"999", 156
"1080", 156, 157-158
"1224", 141
"1746", 59, 158

Origen, 34, 63, 116

Osiris, 9, 16, 132

Our Lady of Fatima, 48

Pan Tadeuz, 47

paradise, 37

Parzival, 17, 96

Pentecost, 14-16, 18, 21, 55

Peter the Hermit, 82

Peyrepertuse, 29

phoenix, 95

Pisces, 26 (see also Age of Pisces; Fishes)

Plato, 156, 158

Pope
  Gregory I, 62
  John Paul I, 46-47, 66-67, 69, 163
  John Paul II, xiv, 7-9, 47-51, 53, 135, 149, 162
  Paul VI, 46

Practice of the Presence of God, The, 72

Priory of Sion, 142

Prophets (Hebrew)
  Daniel, 45, 69
  Ezekiel, 45, 54, 85, 146
  Haggai, 61
  Hosea, 147
  Isaiah, 23, 48-50, 53, 60, 63, 72, 82, 86, 115, 151
  Jeremiah, 57
  Zechariah, 45

Provence, 15, 27, 114, 116, 118, 151

Psalm "89", 87

Rachel, 147-148

Ram, the (Age of Aries), 130

Revelation, (Book of), 123, 127, 129

Rocamadour, 11

Roland, 82

Romans (Paul's Epistle to), 134-135

Rosa, 31, 33

Ruth, 86

Sacred Marriage, xi, 25, 52, 123, 139, 141-142, 149, 158
  blueprint rejected, xv

eclipse symbol, 8, 51
  in Ladyhawke, 36
  in Aquinas, 70
  of fire and water, 90

Saint-Maximin, 58

Saints
  Augustine, 127
  Bernard of Clairvaux, 6, 34, 63
  Bridget, 16
  Francis of Assisi, 31
  Helena, 56
  James, 125
  Malachy, 8, 36
  Paul, 17, 42, 60, 126, 131-132, 134-135, 139
  Peter, 20, 21, 117, 119-120, 129
  Sarah (the Egyptian), 13, 63, 113
  Thomas Aquinas, 70
  Thomas á Becket, 33
  Victor, 13-15, 28

Samson, 88

sangraal, 17, 66

Sarah (wife of Abraham), 146

Secret Garden, The, 149

Shekinah, the, 26, 150

Sister-Bride, 7, 9, 24, 26, 33, 145, 156

Sistine Chapel, 108

Slowacki, Julius, 47, 162-163

Sol Invictus, 126

Solidarity, 48-49

Solomon, 56, 157

Song of Solomon, 26, 31-32, 52, 61, 121

Song of Songs, 9, 24, 27, 31-33, 36-37, 62, 70, 76, 141, 146 (see also Song of Solomon; Canticle of Canticles)

Sophia, 76
Spirit Lake, 53-54, 57
Syndicate of Waters, 112

Tammuz, 24, 132
Tarot trump(s), 82-83, 87
  Charioteer, The, 83
  Devil, The, 86
  Fool, The, 88
  Hanged Man, The, 84
  Hermit, The, 82
  Lovers, The, 85
  Strength, 86
  Tower, The, 87
tekton, 60
Templars, 29, 83, 118 (*see also* Knights
  Templar; Knights of the Temple of
  Solomon)
  tortured Templar, 84-85
Temple of Solomon, 49, 60, 153
Temple, 45, 59-60
Tertullian, 127
Theodosius, 56˙
Thunder Perfect Mind, The, 26
Torah, the, xii, 21
trompe, 82
Tubman, Harriet, 138

Venus, 38
Vesica Piscis, 16, 140, 152, 159-160
Vézelay, 5-7, 11,13, 28
Vine, the, 85-86
Virgin Mary, 10, 27, 33, 35, 76, 146,
  152 (*see also* Blessed Mother)
  Co-Redemptrix, xiv, 52, 135, 150
  in Goddess image, 38

Virgo, 26-27
von Eschenbach, Wolfram, 17
vulva, 140, 159

watchtower, 9, 15, 72, 87, 147-148
watermarks, 78
Western Wall, 56
Wisdom, 32
Wotyla, Karol, 47-48 (*see also* Pope
  John Paul II)
Wounded Knee, 89

Yallop, David, 66, 68
yang, 129, 157
yin, 157

zodiac, 26, 124, 127, 130-131

ABOUT THE AUTHOR

Margaret Leonard Starbird is the author of *The Woman with the Alabaster Jar* and *The Goddess in the Gospels*. Her work provides overwhelming evidence for the union of Christ and Mary Magdalene—the "Sacred Marriage" at the heart of the Christian Gospels.

Starbird is a wife and mother of five children, now grown. She holds a master's degree from the University of Maryland and has studied at the Christian Albrechts Universität in Kiel, Germany, and at Vanderbilt Divinity School in Nashville, Tennessee. She is a teacher of mathematics and language basic skills in an adult education program and gives frequent lectures, retreats, and workshops around the United States and abroad. Her work centers around reclaiming the sacred feminine and the partnership paradigm indigenous to Christianity.

BOOKS OF RELATED INTEREST

THE WOMAN WITH THE ALABASTER JAR
Mary Magdalen and the Holy Grail
by Margaret Starbird

MAGDALENE'S LOST LEGACY
Symbolic Numbers and the Sacred Union in Christianity
by Margaret Starbird

THE GOSPEL OF MARY MAGDALENE
by Jean-Yves Leloup

THE CHURCH OF MARY MAGDALENE
The Sacred Feminine and the Treasure of Rennes-le-Château
by Jean Markale

THE CHALICE OF MAGDALENE
The Search for the Cup That Held the Blood of Christ
by Graham Phillips

THE PATH OF THE PRIESTESS
A Guidebook for Awakening the Divine Feminine
by Sharron Rose

THE SECRET DOWRY OF EVE
Woman's Role in the Development of Consciousness
by Glynda-Lee Hoffmann

THE GODDESS IN INDIA
The Five Faces of the Eternal Feminine
by Devdutt Pattanaik

Inner Traditions • Bear & Company
P.O. Box 388
Rochester, VT 05767
1-800-246-8648
www.InnerTraditions.com

Or contact your local bookseller